Using Lotus® 1-2-3® Release 2.2

Nelda Shelton

South Campus
Tarrant County Junior College District

Sharon Burton

Brookhaven College
Dallas County Community College District

HOUGHTON MIFFLIN COMPANY   BOSTON

Dallas Geneva, Illinois Palo Alto Princeton, New Jersey

Publisher's Foreword

This book is in the Houghton Mifflin Software Solutions Series. The series is explicitly designed to offer solutions to the problems encountered by educators who wish to include instruction on popular commercial application software programs as a component of courses they teach.

The purpose of this series is to provide high quality, inexpensive—in fact, remarkably inexpensive—tutorial manuals keyed to the leading software packages available.

Instructionally Innovative

Each manual in the Software Solutions Series focuses on those features of a particular program that will actually be used by most individuals. The manuals do not purport to teach everything there is to know about the product; to do that, the manual would have to be needlessly complex and would impose unrealistic time constraints on both students and instructors. The manuals will enable students to attain comfortable proficiency in the use of software products.

Flexible

The Software Solutions Series permits instructors to choose the manuals that best suit their needs. This offers an important advantage over those manuals that combine coverage of several programs in a single publication and thus limit flexibility.

Cost

Students enrolled in a computer literacy or business data processing course often require lab-based instruction on the use of three or more application programs, usually a word processing program, a database manager, and a spreadsheet program. This common course configuration can impose a financial burden on students if they must purchase three expensive manuals in addition to the primary course text. We believe the Software Solutions Series goes a long way toward solving this problem by providing an effective and inexpensive method for learning about software.

High Quality

All manuals in the Software Solutions Series are authored by writers who have teaching experience in the classroom and in training programs in business and industry. Each manual in the series has been reviewed for accuracy and pedagogical effectiveness.

Software Disks

The Software Solutions Series currently consists of fourteen manuals and the following software products.

Master disks containing educational versions of V-P Planner Plus, Microsoft Works, WordPerfect 4.2, WordStar, dBASE III Plus, and SuperCalc 4 are available form Houghton Mifflin without charge to adopters of the manuals. These disks may be duplicated for individual student use by instructors in accordance with applicable license agreements.

For Lotus 1-2-3, WordPerfect 5.0, Microsoft Word, MS-DOS, dBASE IV, Lotus 1-2-3 Release 2.2, BASIC and PageMaker, data disks rather than educational versions of the program disks are available from Houghton Mifflin without charge to adopters.

All manuals in the Software Solutions Series are for use with IBM equipment except for PageMaker, which is only for the Macintosh.

We wish to thank Microsoft Corporation, WordPerfect Corporation, MicroPro International, Computer Associates, Ashton-Tate and Paperback Software for their cooperation in helping us make this series available.

Preface

Using Lotus 1-2-3 Release 2.2 introduces the student to one of the best and most popular spreadsheet application programs available today. The package makes it easy for students to learn the basics of Lotus 1-2-3 in a very short time. It does so by encouraging the natural learning process so that students avoid frustration and confusion. This sharp focus allows students to develop an understanding of how Lotus 1-2-3 works and to issue commands confidently to achieve useful results—all within a manageable time frame.

Pedagogical features that ensure rapid mastery of the basics are integral to each chapter.

- An introduction explains features covered in the chapter.
- New terminology is presented at the beginning of each chapter.
- Step-by-step instructions are followed by an illustrated example and practice exercises that allow students to use each feature in a hands-on environment.
- Every exercise step number is enclosed in a box, making it easy for students to identify what they are to read and what they are to do.
- Frequent illustrations make it easy for students to check their work as they go along, building their confidence and understanding and providing positive reinforcement.
- Tips give students important shortcuts and reminders as well as directions and explanations.

- Each chapter ends with a summary of the concepts and commands presented in the chapter; this encourages review and mastery of the basics.
- End of chapter applications offer additional practice on the concepts taught in the chapter.
- Two appendixes provide a summary of commands, information on using a hard disk, and instructions for formatting a floppy disk.

The manual's step-by-step instructions complement the classroom-tested Read and Do approach to teaching. After reading a simple explanation of a new concept and studying an example, students complete an exercise on the computer. This logical presentation means that students focus on one feature at a time; are guided through an exercise in which they practice using feature under discussion; and complete the exercise on their own—gaining confidence as they complete the performance of each new feature. Clear, hands-on instructions walk students through each new element of the program, and illustrations showing correct screens or printed output allow them to check their work as they go along.

Because this manual is designed to enable first-time users to gain reasonable proficiency with the program, the most advanced 1-2-3 features are not covered. Six text chapters teach the basics for setting up a spreadsheet, creating a bar graph, and using 1-2-3's database capabilities.

A master copy of a data disk, which can be copied, is provided to instructors adopting this manual. The disk contains a sample worksheet, so that students can see how the screen is supposed to look and can practice retrieving a worksheet at the outset. Students then create their own worksheet, save it on the data disk, and are given further instructions for modifying the worksheet and creating other files.

A disk with two sample worksheets and a sample graph file has been provided for use with your text exercises. Specific instructions on how and when to use this disk are given in the text. There is space available on this disk for you to create your own worksheets, graphs, and databases, practicing the concepts in this text.

To use this package, you must have the following:

- Lotus 1-2-3 (Release 2.2) and PrintGraph
- An IBM PC or compatible computer that uses double-sided floppy disks
- At least 256K RAM (Random Access Memory)
- MS or PCDOS 2.0 or higher

- Two floppy disk drives or a hard disk system (some instructions may vary)
- Graphics capabilities
- A standard color or black-and-white monitor
- A printer with graphics capabilities if it is to print 1-2-3 graphs. To print graphs, you need a graphics printer or plotter supported by Lotus 1-2-3.
- A copy of the master data disk provided to instructors adopting this manual
- Formatted floppy disks for backing up the data disk and storing data, if desired

Acknowledgments

In writing textbook materials, authors need the help of a number of individuals.

We would like to thank Judy Ivy, Tarrant County Junior College, for her tips and attention to detail. Her many hours spent working through the manuscript are greatly appreciated.

Contents

x   **Contents**

1

Learning About
Your PC

Welcome to the personal computer and Lotus 1-2-3! In this text we will be discussing (with a few exceptions) the same basic information covered in the Lotus 1-2-3 manual.

So that you will be more efficient in learning to use Lotus 1-2-3, take a few minutes to get acquainted with your personal computer. Refer to your PC's guide to operations, to the DOS manual, and to any other training materials you have, for specific instructions on its use. Don't be intimidated by the computer. It's simply a sophisticated tool that saves time and improves your efficiency and productivity in handling information.

Before you begin you should know that learning to use Lotus 1-2-3 on your PC involves both paying attention to detail and practicing. As a first step in that process, this chapter will acquaint you with the basic terminology and components of your computer system.

Terminology

Knowing the following basic terms will help you understand the PC and its operation:

Hardware means the physical parts of the computer.

Peripheral equipment includes all the parts of the computer other than the central processing unit (the brains of the computer), such as the keyboard, the monitor, and the printer. Peripheral equipment is in the category of hardware.

Software means the programs that run on the computer.

Programs are sets of instructions that tell the computer what to do, when to do it, and how to do it. In this case, the software is Lotus 1-2-3. This software allows you to fill a spreadsheet, create graphics, and use database management. Other software allows the computer to perform other tasks.

The **prompt** is shown on your screen as >, preceded by the letter of the disk drive you are using. It alerts you that the computer has been activated and is waiting for further instructions.

Commands are combinations of keystrokes that you use to instruct the computer to perform certain functions.

Functions are operations performed by the computer.

We will introduce additional terms as we go through this chapter.

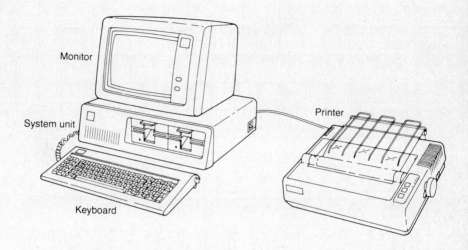

Figure 1-1 Basic components of the PC.

Basic Components of the PC

The PC has four basic components that work together as a complete system: the keyboard, the monitor, the system unit, and the printer. These components are shown in Figure 1-1. You should become familiar with the functions and capabilities of each of them.

Keyboard

The PC keyboard looks like the keyboard of a typewriter, except that it has additional keys. The **keyboard** lets you interact with the computer. The two basic types of keyboards common among PCs are PC/XT and AT enhanced keyboards (IBM System/2 keyboards are similar to the AT). Figure 1-2 shows both types.

You can see from Figure 1-2 that the central portion of the PC/XT keyboard has the standard display of letters and numbers. To the left are 10 additional keys known as special function keys (F keys). To the right is a numeric keypad that can be used for quick keyboarding of numbers or to move the cell pointer around, as you will see.

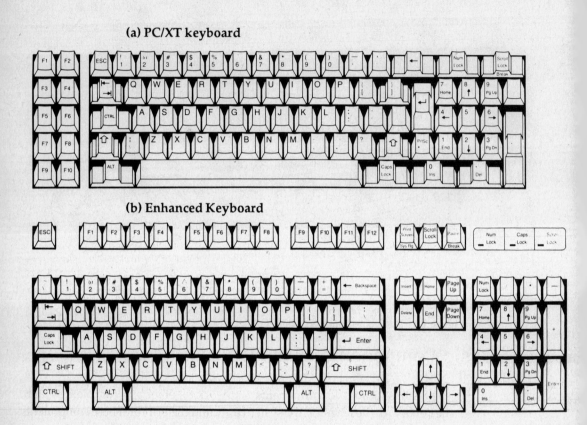

(a) PC/XT keyboard

(b) Enhanced Keyboard

Figure 1-2 PC/XT and AT Enhanced Keyboards.

The **special function keys** make the system perform particular commands, thus eliminating the need to press several keys to execute these commands. These F keys are discussed in later chapters and are listed in Appendix A. They are located at the top on the AT enhanced keyboard.

Complete the following steps with a computer keyboard in front of you:

1 Determine the type of keyboard you have attached to your computer.

Keyboard:_____

2 Take a few moments to locate these additional keys:

The **Escape (Esc)** key is used to break or cancel a function or instruction. It cancels the last entry in a command path.

The **Tab** (←→) key is located under the Esc key. This key moves the cursor to the next tab setting.

The **Control (Ctrl)** key is used in combination with other keys to give the computer particular instructions. For example, Ctrl-C and ^C both mean "Press the Control key, keep it down, and then press the C key."

The **left shift** (⇑) key is located under the Ctrl key. This key is held down to capitalize letters or to obtain special characters or symbols on the tops of the keys.

The **Alternate (Alt)** key, located under the left shift key, is used in Lotus 1-2-3 to release the system when it locks or "freezes." The Alt key can perform this function only if Lotus 1-2-3 is active. When the system refuses to perform, press the Ctrl, Alt, and Del keys all together. If the Ctrl-Alt-Del combination is pressed, all data not saved are lost. The Alt key is also used with other keys to create macros. A **macro** is a keyboard command that can be used to simplify functions. Macros are not covered in this version of Lotus 1-2-3.

The **Backspace** (←) key moves the cursor back one space and deletes any character it goes over.

The **Enter or Return** (↵) key is used (1) to complete an instruction you have given to the computer or (2) to enter data.

The **right shift** (⇑) key is located to the right of the question mark/diagonal key. This key is held down to capitalize letters or to obtain special characters or symbols on the tops of the keys.

The **CapsLock** key works somewhat differently than a typewriter's Caps-Lock key. This key allows you to type capital letters and numbers without using the shift keys. For example, when CapsLock is on, you can type A1B2C3D4 without having the special characters above 1, 2, 3, and 4 appear. When CapsLock is on, Lotus displays CAPS at the bottom of the screen.

To the right of the Backspace key are additional special keys, including the numeric keypad. With Lotus 1-2-3, you can use the numeric keypad to enter numbers by pressing the **Number Lock (NumLock)** key or by holding down a shift key. You can also use the numeric keypad to move the cell pointer (this will be explained in the next chapter). Locate these additional keys on your keyboard.

When NumLock is pressed, Lotus displays NUM at the bottom of the screen, and you can enter numbers from the numeric keypad.

The **Print Screen (PrtSc)** key is used to dump (send) to the printer whatever appears on the screen. This key is not used as a Lotus 1-2-3 command but is convenient to use at times. If you press the PrtSc key, an asterisk (*) appears on the screen. However, if you hold down the left or right shift key and also press the PrtSc key, the data on the screen will be dumped, that is, printed if your printer is on.

The **Insert (Ins)** key lets you type over characters while in EDIT mode.

The **Delete (Del)** key erases the character at the current cell-pointer position while in EDIT mode. Text to the right of the cursor moves left.

Monitor

The **monitor**, also called the screen, display, or CRT (cathode ray tube), looks like a television screen—as you can see in Figure 1-1. The monitor displays both the data that you keyboard and instructions for you to follow. A PC monitor has 24 horizontal lines of 80 spaces each. Just as there are different types of keyboards, there are different types of monitors. Monitors are either monochrome (black-and-white, phosphorous, amber) or color. There are at least two knobs on a monitor: one knob adjusts the screen contrast, the other controls the screen brightness for eye comfort.

Complete the following step with your monitor:

1. Determine the type of monitor you are using.

Monitor type: _____

System Unit

The **system unit** houses the **central processing unit (CPU)**, the "brains" of the computer. The system unit also contains the memory unit, one or more disk drives, the power supply, and other important hardware. See Figure 1-3.

Memory

As its name implies, **memory** stores data temporarily in your computer until you decide to save (record) them on a disk. Your PC has at least 256K of memory, or storage space for at least 262,144 characters. Note that part of this memory is taken up by Lotus 1-2-3 itself.

Additional memory makes it easier to complete some of the advanced functions performed by Lotus 1-2-3.

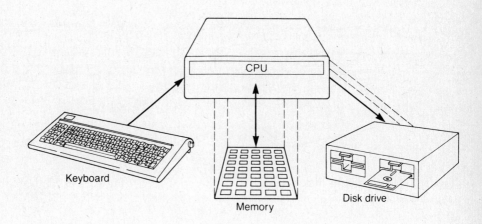

Figure 1-3 System unit.

Complete the following step about your computer's memory:

1 How much memory does your computer have?

Memory capacity: _____

Disk Drive

A disk drive holds the disks. A **disk drive** writes (records) information onto a disk from memory and reads (plays) information from the disk back into memory.

If a computer has two disk drives, they are usually called drive A and drive B, although no labels appear on them. Full-height drives are arranged side by side, with A on the left and B on the right, as shown in Figure 1-4. Half-height drives are stacked with A on top of B, as shown in Figure 1-5.

Complete the following step to determine your type of disk drive:

1 Determine the type of disk drive installation in your computer system. Check one of the following:

a. One hard disk drive with one floppy disk drive _____

b. Two floppy disk drives _____

c. One hard disk drive with two floppy drives _____

The disk drives of a PC are almost always double-sided, double- or high density. That is, they read information from and write it onto both sides of the disk.

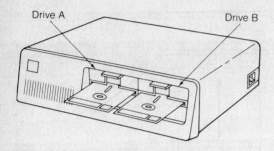

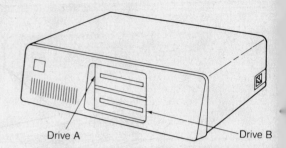

Figure 1-4 Full-height disk drives.   **Figure 1-5** Half-height disk drives.

The drive in use is known as the **logged disk drive**. For example, if the computer is reading data from drive A, then drive A is the logged disk drive. The disk inserted in that drive is the logged disk. The red light on the disk drive goes on when that drive is writing or reading data.

Disk Operating System

The computer's **disk operating system (DOS)** manages the way in which data are entered onto or moved from the disk. DOS is the intermediary between the software (Lotus 1-2-3) and the hardware (the PC). Lotus 1-2-3 requires that DOS be loaded in your computer first. For instance, without DOS, Lotus cannot communicate with the peripheral equipment—monitor, printer, and disk drives.

Disks

The **disk**, also known as a diskette or floppy disk, is a magnetic recording medium. The disk can be 5 1/4 inches or 3 1/2 inches in diameter. The 5 1/4-inch, double-sided disk can hold either 327,680 or 368,640 characters, depending on the disk drive used. In other words, a double-sided disk can hold 320K or 360K. Figure 1-6 illustrates the components of a disk.

The write-protect notch allows information to be written onto the disk. If the notch is covered with a write-protect tab (for a 5 1/4" disk), you cannot write (save) information on the disk, but you can read information from it. When the notch is covered with a tab, nothing on the disk can be changed. The disk drive uses the index hole to keep track of where the data are on the disk; that is, of what part of the disk is being used.

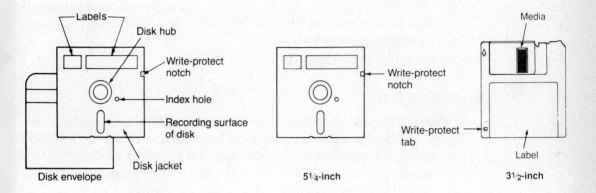

Figure 1-6 5 1/4- and 3 1/2-inch diskettes.

A hard disk may be used with your computer to accommodate large amounts of data and permanent storage of programs and files. A hard disk is made of rigid magnetic material, whereas a floppy disk is somewhat flexible.

Complete the following step to identify the type of disks you will be using while learning Lotus 1-2-3.

1 Determine which type of disks you will be using and place a check in the appropriate blank.

5-1/4-inch _____ 3-1/2-inch _____

Care of Disks

Disks must be handled with extreme care to prevent damage to them or to any information stored on them. Follow these steps in caring for your 5 1/4" disks:

1. Keep disks in their protective envelopes when they are not being used.
2. Avoid bending disks.
3. Store disks away from extreme heat and away from any piece of equipment that might contain a magnet, such as a magnetic paper-clip holder or a telephone.
4. Carefully insert disks into the disk drive to avoid jamming them; make certain that the label is toward you and that the write-protect notch is to the left.
5. Never insert disks into the disk drive while turning the system on or off, while printing, or while the drive is running.

6. Do not exert pressure on disks. Either place a blank label on the disk and then write its name on the label, using a felt-tip pen, or write on the label before putting it on the disk.
7. Do not touch the exposed recording surface.

Formatting a Disk

Before you can use a new disk, it must be formatted. Formatting a disk means preparing the disk to record information. Procedures for formatting a disk are presented in Appendix B. If your instructor has given you the data disk that accompanies this text, DO NOT format this disk. Formatting a disk erases the data stored on a disk as well as preparing it to receive data.

Printer

A **printer** is like a typewriter in that it prints data on paper. The paper printout is called a **hard copy.** Both have similar parts—a platen, a paper bail, and a paper release. However, a typewriter prints each character as you enter it, whereas a printer prints data only after you have entered all the characters.

There are two basic types of printers: text printers and graphics printers (or plotters). You may use separate printers to print text and graphics, or you may be able to use the same printer for both. Text printers include dot matrix, daisy-wheel, laser, and inkjet printers. Graphics printers include dot matrix, laser, and inkjet printers.

Summary

Hardware means the physical parts of the computer.

Software means the programs, or sets of instructions, that run the computer.

Programs tell the computer what to do, when to do it, and how to do it.

Peripheral equipment includes the keyboard, monitor, printer, and other attachments.

The monitor is also known as a screen, display, or CRT.

The system unit houses the central processing unit (CPU).

Memory stores data temporarily until they are saved on a disk.

The logged disk drive is the disk drive in use.

DOS is the PC's disk operating system, which manages the way data are written to and read from the disk. DOS also performs other tasks, such as printing and storing files.

Disks are the magnetic recording medium for the computer.

Writing (or saving) means recording information onto a disk.

Reading means playing information from the disk into memory.

Formatting means preparing a new disk to record data.

A hard copy is a paper printout of the output of a computer.

2

Getting Started

What is Lotus 1-2-3? Lotus 1-2-3 Release 2.2 is a powerful integrated software package that combines a spreadsheet with graphics and a database management program. The spreadsheet (also called a worksheet) displayed on the monitor is divided into columns and rows. Using the computer, you can enter values, headings, formulas, or totals in the spreadsheet.

Even a simple spreadsheet combined with text and graphics can be a useful tool in decision making. Using formulas, Lotus 1-2-3 can complete calculations to provide information for forecasting, profit and loss analysis, investments, sales analysis, budgeting, inventories, and many more business applications.

Booting up Your PC with a Floppy Disk

NOTE: If you are using a hard disk DOS, the Lotus 1-2-3 system has probably already been loaded on the hard disk. If not, your instructor will tell you how to load DOS and Lotus 1-2-3.

Boot up means to activate the computer. The PC must be started with the DOS disk in drive A. (If you have a hard disk, this is usually not necessary). Use the following steps to start up your PC, if you have a single or double-disk system:

1. Hold the DOS disk so that the exposed oval slot points away from you and the label faces you, on top.

2. Carefully slide the disk all the way into drive A, then close the drive door.

3. Turn your computer on. Be sure to turn on your monitor as well.

4. The computer's power switch is the red switch on the unit's right side. Flip it up to turn the unit on (see Figure 2-1). When the computer is loading a disk, the in-use light comes on. Do not open a disk drive if the in-use light is on.

5. If you have a color monitor, turn it on with the top knob. (The monochrome monitor goes on automatically.) Use the other knobs to adjust the screen's contrast and brightness. Turn the knobs clockwise to increase the brightness and contrast; turn them counterclockwise to decrease the brightness and contrast.

6. To restart the computer when it is already on, press and hold down, in this order, Ctrl, Alt, Del. Then release all three keys.

TIP: Use the command Ctrl-Alt-Del to restart the system only when the power is already on. Do not use this command to restart the system when you are making changes in data, because the changes you have made will not be saved.

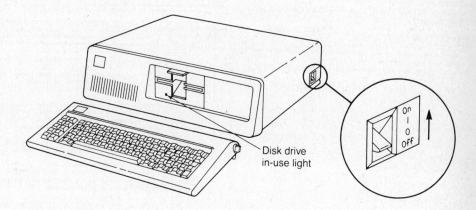

Figure 2-1 On-off switch and in-use light.

7 Respond to the date and time requests, pressing Enter after each one. The A> prompt will appear on your screen.

8 The blinking light on your screen is the cell pointer, or cursor. Like the printing point on a typewriter, it marks your position and moves to the right as you enter data.

9 To enter the date, use the month-day-year format, separating the numbers with dashes or slashes. For the number 1, use the top-row number 1. Never use the letter *l* for the number 1. Press Enter after the date is entered. Enter the date in one of the following ways: 3/14/90 or 03/14/90; 3-14-90 or 03-14-90.

10 Key the correct hour and minute, using the colon. The PC uses a 24-hour clock. For example, 8:10 means 8:10 A.M.; 20:10 means 8:10 P.M. Press Enter after the time is entered.

11 The screen will show the following prompt: A>

Starting Lotus 1-2-3 with a Floppy Disk

NOTE: If you are using a hard disk, the Lotus system has probably been installed on it. Your instructor will tell you how to start Lotus.

You have two choices when starting Lotus 1-2-3: (1) you may start 1-2-3 directly from the operating system prompt, which saves time and computer memory space,

To load Lotus 1-2-3 with a floppy disk from the operating system prompt:

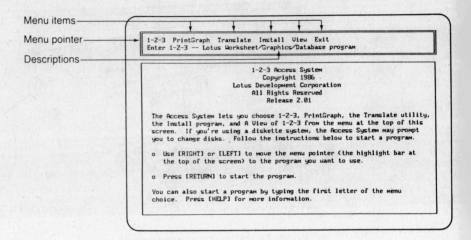

Menu items ─────

Menu pointer ─────

Descriptions ─────

Figure 2-2   Access System menu.

1. Remove the DOS or other disk from drive A and replace it with the Lotus 1-2-3 disk.

2. Key: 123.

3. Press Enter. The Lotus 1-2-3 title appears. A blank spreadsheet appears.

    or (2) you may start 1-2-3 through the Access System, which allows you to use the Access System Menu to select other programs. For this text's purposes, you will start 1-2-3 through the Access System.

    The Access System Menu is shown in Figure 2-2. The Access System Menu displays a number of companion programs. You can easily switch back and forth between Lotus 1-2-3 and these companion programs.

    PrintGraph is the program you use to print or plot graphs created and saved during a 1-2-3 session. This program allows you to select the color, type style (font), density (number of dots per character), and position of the graph on paper.

    Translate lets you move data from 1-2-3 to other programs.

    Install lets you tell 1-2-3 what equipment you have to perform specific functions.

    Exit allows you to leave the Access System Menu and return to DOS.

    You can cancel your choice made from the menu by pressing the Esc (Escape) key. Pressing Esc will return you to the Access System Menu.

Use the following steps to start Lotus 1-2-3 from the Access System Menu using a floppy system:

1   Remove the DOS disk from drive A and replace it with the Lotus 1-2-3 System Disk.

2   Place your data disk in drive B.

3   Key lotus. It doesn't matter if you key lotus in upper or lowercase letters or in any combination. The computer will accept any combination of letters.

4   Press Enter. The Access System Menu appears.

5   Press Enter with 1-2-3 highlighted. Wait. The Lotus 1-2-3 copyright notice appears. Because 1-2-3 was highlighted, all that was necessary to start Lotus was to press Enter. Another method of starting Lotus is to key 1 (the numeral from the top-row keys). A blank 1-2-3 spreadsheet appears on your screen.

Reading the Spreadsheet Screen

Figure 2-3 shows a spreadsheet as it might be set up to project sales. The Lotus spreadsheet is set up to make placement of each piece of information relatively easy.

SALES PROJECTIONS			
SOFTWARE	1987	1988	1989
WordStar	$20,000	$30,000	$39,000
MultiMate-ADVII	23,000	29,000	37,000
WordPerfect	22,500	29,500	36,790
Totals	$65,500	$88,500	$112,790

Figure 2-3 Sample spreadsheet in Lotus 1-2-3.

The spreadsheet consists of the following parts: control panel, border, spreadsheet rows and columns, date and time indicator, and other status indicators, such as NUM and UNDO. Study Figure 2-4.

1. The control panel consists of four areas: cell address, mode indicator, entry line, and prompt line. These areas are shown in Figure 2-5.

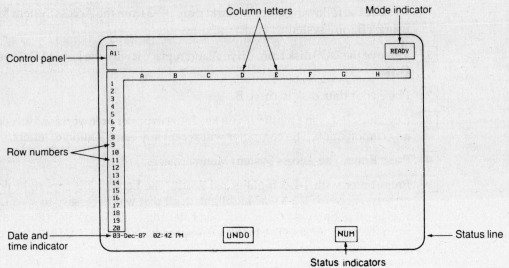

Figure 2-4 Parts of the spreadsheet.

a. The cell address displays the location of the cell where your cursor or cell pointer is currently located.

b. The mode indicator displays the current mode of operation, such as READY, EDIT, MENU, or HELP. There are 14 mode indicators. This manual will help you become familiar with the most commonly used mode indicators. The mode is highlighted and appears in the upper-right corner of your screen.

c. The entry line contains any data you enter, as well as information already entered. The data you enter are not placed in the cell or on the status line until you press Enter or an arrow key. Therefore, you may edit (revise) your data as you enter them. The entry line displays the Main Menu—a list of 1-2-3 commands that appears when you press slash (/) in READY mode, as shown in Figure 2-4.

d. The prompt line contains information, an explanation of specific commands, or a submenu.

2. The rows and columns form the border of the spreadsheet. The numbers listed vertically on the left side of the screen are called row numbers. The letters listed across the top are called column letters.

TIP: The computer beeps when you try to move the cell pointer beyond the border of the spreadsheet (above or to the left of row 1).

Figure 2-5 Control panel.

3. The spreadsheet is the grid, or matrix, consisting of 8,192 rows (numbered 1 through 8,192) and 256 columns (labeled A through IV). Other important components of the spreadsheet include the cell, the cell pointer, and the window.

    a. The cell is the unit of the spreadsheet, at the intersection of a column and a row, that can store data. For example, cell address B3 is the intersection of column B and row 3.

    b. The cell pointer, or cursor, marks the highlighted position at the intersection where data will appear. The cell pointer can be moved to any cell in the spreadsheet. The cell where the cell pointer is currently located is called the *current cell*.

    c. The window is all the information displayed on your screen in rows 1 through 20. The number of columns displayed may vary, however, because the column width can be changed. The default global column width of 9 characters lets you see 8 columns (A through H) at a time. However, you can change the column width to any size, from 0 to 240 characters. The window may contain your spreadsheet, data management information, a graph, or any information related to what you are working on.

4. The date and time indicator displays the date and time, based on what you entered at the operating system prompt or on what the computer's internal clock supplied. You can change this indicator using the Worksheet Global Default Other Clock command. A message will appear on this line as you work with 1-2-3. For example, the following message will be displayed when you enter an improper cell number: Invalid cell or range address.

5. The status indicators appear on the lower-right corner of the screen on the status line, to indicate a particular program condition or key condition. For example, when the NUM indicator appears, it indicates that the NumLock key has been pressed. When NUM is on, you can use the numeric keypad to enter numbers. The most common status indicators are listed in Appendix A.

6. The UnDo indicator will undo your last action. For instance, if you accidentally erase something from a cell, you can press Alt and F4 to bring back what was erased.

Displaying Mode Indicators

Mode indicators appear individually in caps in the upper-right corner of the control panel. Each indicator tells you the mode in which 1-2-3 is currently operating. Notice that you are in READY mode on the screen you are viewing.

You will learn more about these modes as you begin to use them, in Chapter 3. The most commonly used mode indicators are listed in Figure 2-6.

Mode	Action
EDIT	You are editing an entry.
ERROR	An error has occurred; press Esc or Return to clear it.
FILES	A menu of files is being displayed.
FIND	You selected /Data Query Find to search for a record that matched your criteria.
FRMT	You selected /Data Format Line Edit to edit a format line.
HELP	You have requested help.
LABEL	You are entering a label (text) to be placed in a cell.
MENU	A command menu is displayed, and you are selecting a command from it.
NAMES	A menu of existing range names or graph names is being displayed.
POINT	The cell pointer is pointing to a cell or range of cells.
READY	1-2-3 is ready for you to enter data or a command.
STAT	Worksheet status information is being displayed.
VALUE	You are entering a number or a formula to be placed in a cell.
WAIT	A command or process is in progress and 1-2-3 cannot accept another operation.

Figure 2-6 Commonly used mode indicators.

Moving Around the Spreadsheet

When it comes to moving the cell pointer around the spreadsheet, Lotus 1-2-3 makes full use of the keyboard. The cell pointer can be moved in the READY, POINT, MENU, and HELP modes.

NumLock Key: A Status Indicator

The NumLock key, located above the numeric keypad, toggles (turns on and off) the number keys of the numeric keypad. When NumLock is on, the arrow keys, shown in Figure 2-7, cannot be used to move the cell pointer around the spreadsheet.

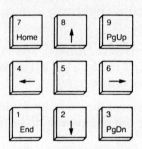

Figure 2-7 Numeric keyboard.

To view the NumLock status indicator, follow these steps:

1   Press NumLock once. Notice that NUM appears on the status line in the lower-right corner of your screen.

2   Press NumLock again to turn it off.

Moving One Cell at a Time

You can move the cell pointer one cell at a time by using one of the arrow keys on the numeric keypad or cursor pad. Locate these keys on your keyboard as you study Figure 2-7.

Watch the top line (cell address) of the control panel change as you move the cell pointer through the following steps:

1   Press → to move the cell pointer to the right.

2   Press ← to move the cell pointer to the left.

3   Press ↓ to move the cell pointer down.

4   Press ↑ to move the cell pointer up.

Notice that the cell pointer highlights the current cell in the control panel. It designates the cell eligible to receive data.

Moving One Window at a Time

Move one window at a time by using the following keys. Watch the cell address change as you use these keys.

1 To move right one window (called a *big right*) in the READY and POINT modes, hold down Ctrl and press → (or use the Tab key by itself). (In the EDIT mode, a big right moves the window right only five characters.) The cell pointer should be in I1.

2 To move left one window (a *big left*) in the READY and POINT modes, hold down Ctrl and press ←. (In the EDIT mode, a big left moves the window left five characters.) The cell pointer should be in A1.

3 Press PgDn (Page Down). PgDn moves the window down, to let you view a lower part of the spreadsheet. The cell pointer should be in A21.

4 Press PgUp (Page Up). PgUp moves the window up, to let you view a higher portion of the spreadsheet. The cell pointer should be in A1.

Moving Many Windows at a Time

You can move many windows at a time by using GoTo or Home, or by using End in combination with an arrow key. To move around the spreadsheet, use these keys.

To use GoTo (F5), follow these steps:

1 Press F5.

2 At the prompt, enter the cell address to go to, using the column letter and row number. Key: C4 as the desired cell address.

3 Press Enter. The C4 cell will be highlighted.

TIP: If you press F5, enter a number without a letter; and press Enter, the program beeps and displays a message at the bottom of the screen. The message reads Invalid cell or range address. The ERROR mode indicator appears flashing in the upper right corner of your screen. Press Esc to delete the incorrect cell address.

Using Pointer-Movement Keys in Ready, Point, Menu, and Help Modes

Figure 2-8 lists and describes the keys that move the pointer in READY, POINT, MENU, and HELP modes.

Key	READY and POINT Modes
←, →, ↑, or ↓	Moves one cell left, right, up, or down
Ctrl/← or →	Moves one window left or right
PgUp/PgDn	Moves one window up or down
Home	Moves to upper left corner
End/Home	Moves to lower right corner where you have last entered data
End/↑ or ↓	Moves up or down to filled cell at next intersection of blank or filled cell
End/← or →	Moves left or right to filled cell at next intersection of blank or filled cell

Key	MENU and HELP Modes
← or →	Moves one cell left or right
↑ or ↓	Moves up or down one item in HELP mode
↑ or ↓	Beeps in MENU mode
Home	Moves to first item
End	Moves to last item

Figure 2-8   Pointer-movement keys.

Changing or Correcting Data on the Entry Line

You can change or correct data with the pointer-movement keys in Figure 2-9.

Watch the entry line as you practice the following changes:

1. Press Home.

2. Press F5 (GoTo).

3. At the entry line A1, key: C7 (without any punctuation).

4. Press Backspace twice to erase C7.

5. Key: C4 (without any punctuation).

6 Press Esc to cancel the entry.

7 Key: C5 (press Ctrl Break).

TIP: Lotus 1-2-3 uses the F2 function key to initiate EDIT mode, so that you can change the contents of a cell without reentering all the characters. By using the F2 key, you can modify the cell contents by inserting or deleting characters.

Backspace, Esc, and Ctrl-Break can all be used to correct mistakes on the entry line.

Key	Action
Backspace	Corrects mistakes while you are making a cell entry. Backspace to correct entry; retype entry.
Enter	Corrects mistakes after you have completed an entry. Move cell pointer to cell that you want to change; type correct entry; press Enter .
Esc	Clears entire entry in a cell before Enter is pressed; cancels a menu selection.
Ctrl/Break	Interrupts an entry and returns you to READY mode.

Figure 2-9 Keys for changing or correcting data.

Getting Help

Lotus 1-2-3 provides an on-line Help mode that displays information about the specific area of the program you are in, different kinds of errors, and various 1-2-3 commands. To display the Help screen, press the F1 function key. To choose additional information about a topic, use the pointer-movement keys to point to a topic, then press Enter.

To become familiar with the Help mode, try the following commands: (If using a two-disk floppy system, insert Help disk **before** pressing F1.)

1 Press F1 to display the Help screen.

2 Select a topic that interests you. Press the down arrow to move the menu pointer to the desired topic. (The menu pointer is the cursor highlighting a choice in the menu.)

3 Press Enter.

4 Press Esc when you have completed your browsing.

Selecting a Command from the Main Menu

To select a command from the Main Menu, you press the forward slash (/) key. The Main Menu of commands appears on the entry line. You then enter a command by keying the first letter of the word representing the command. For example, to quit the spreadsheet, all you need to do is key Q for *Quit*.

If you make a wrong selection, press Esc.

A Lotus 1-2-3 Session

Let's learn how to enter data in the spreadsheet, save the spreadsheet as a file, and clear the screen. You will learn more about each procedure in later chapters.

To end a session, use the following steps:

1. Be sure a blank screen is displayed.

2. Move the cell pointer to A1, if it isn't already there, by pressing Home.

3. Key your first name and press the right arrow key. The cell pointer advances to cell B1.

4. Key your middle initial and press the right arrow. The cell pointer advances to cell C1.

5. Key your last name and press Enter. Your name is entered and the pointer remains in the cell.

6. Move the cell pointer to cell A2.

7. Key your city and state. Press the right arrow key. The text may spill over into other cells.

8. To save the file, key: / F (for *File*) S (for *Save*).

9. Before keying the file name, you may need to backspace to delete previous drive information (from A: to B: or from C: to A:).

10. Key: b:prac (Because you are saving the file on the data disk in drive B, you must precede your file name, prac, with b and a colon.) If you are using a hard disk system, key: a:prac

11. Press Enter.

12. To clear the screen, key: / W (for *Worksheet*) E for (*Erase*) Y (for *Yes*). Your screen will be cleared.

Exiting Lotus 1-2-3

Always make sure to save any information you have been working on before exiting Lotus 1-2-3. You will learn more about saving your files in Chapter 3.

To exit Lotus 1-2-3, follow these steps:

1. Key: / (to display the Main Menu).

2. Key: Q (for *Quit*).

3. The control panel now highlights No. Key: Y (for *Yes*). If you want to continue with this session, press Enter to select No.

4. Either (a) the operating system (DOS) prompt will appear, or (b) the Access System screen will appear.

   a. If the DOS prompt appears, remove your disks and turn off your computer. (This prompt appears if you started 1-2-3 from the DOS prompt.)

   b. If the Access System screen appears, key: E (for *Exit*). (This screen appears if you started 1-2-3 from the Access System Menu.) The DOS prompt now appears. Remove your disks and turn off the computer.

TIP | Before you quit, you should be certain that you have saved the spreadsheet if you want to use it again; otherwise, all of your work will be lost.

Summary

To boot up (activate) your system with a floppy disk:

1. Insert DOS into drive A.
2. Close the drive door.
3. Turn your computer on.
4. Respond to the date and time requests, pressing Enter after each one. An A> prompt appears.

To load from the Access System screen with a floppy system:

1. Remove the DOS disk from drive A; replace it with the Lotus 1-2-3 System Disk.
2. Key: lotus.
3. Press Enter. The Access System Menu appears.

4. Press Enter with 1-2-3 highlighted. The Lotus 1-2-3 copyright notice appears. The 1-2-3 spreadsheet appears on your screen.

To view the Main Menu:

Press the slash key (/).

To use arrow keys:

→ Moves cell pointer to the right

← Moves cell pointer to the left

↓ Moves cell pointer down

↑ Moves cell pointer up

To use the GoTo command:

1. Press F5.

2. Key the column and row desired.

3. Press Enter.

To use pointer-movement keys in READY, POINT, MENU, and HELP modes:

Key	READY and POINT Modes
←,→,↑, or ↓	Moves one cell left, right, up, or down
Ctrl/← or →	Moves one window left or right
PgUp/PgDn	Moves one window up or down
Home	Moves to upper-left corner
End/Home	Moves to lower-right corner where you have last entered data
End/ ↑ or ↓	Moves up or down to filled cell at next intersection of blank or filled cell
End/ ← or →	Moves left or right to filled cell at next intersection of blank or filled cell

Key	MENU (press /) and HELP (press F1) modes
← or →	Moves one cell left or right
↑ or ↓	Moves up or down one item in HELP mode
↑ or ↓	Beeps in MENU mode
Home	Moves to first item
End	Moves to last item

To change or correct data:

Key	Action
Backspace	Corrects mistakes while you are making a cell entry. Backspace to correct entry; rekey entry.
Enter	Corrects mistakes after you have completed an entry. Move cell pointer to cell that you want to change; type correct entry; press Enter.
Esc	Clears entire entry in a cell before Enter is pressed; cancels a menu selection.

To get help:

1. Press F1 to display the Help screen.
2. Press the down arrow to move menu pointer to a choice in the menu.
3. Press Enter to continue using menu.
4. Press Esc to leave the Help program.

To select a command from the Main Menu:

1. Key: / (slash key).
2. Key the first letter of the word representing the command.

To exit Lotus 1-2-3:

1. Key: / (to display Main Menu).
2. Key: Q (for *Quit*).
3. Key: Y (for *Yes*).
4. Either (a) the operating system (DOS) prompt will appear, or (b) the Access System screen will appear.

   a. If the DOS prompt appears, remove your disks and turn off your computer.

   b. If the Access System screen appears, key: E (for *Exit*). When the DOS prompt appears, remove your disks and turn off your computer.

Applications

Application 1

Practice the following pointer moves in the READY mode. Move the cell pointer

 1. three cells to the right.
 2. four cells down.
 3. two cells up.
 4. to the upper-left corner of your screen.
 5. to the lower-right corner of your screen.
 6. one window right.
 7. one window left.
 8. one window down.
 9. one window up.
 10. to cell A1.

Application 2

Use the GoTo command to move the cell pointer to the following cells:

 1. C10
 2. S1
 3. B4
 4. I12 (column I row 12)
 5. G40
 6. J2
 7. R25
 8. D5
 9. A1

Application 3

Enter the following data as shown on the entry line; then use the Backspace key to make the necessary changes. **DO NOT** press Enter or a cursor arrow.

 1. Key C9; change it to B9; erase it.
 2. Key the word Lotis; correct the spelling to Lotus; erase it.

3. Key the words Sales Report; change to SALES REPORT; erase.

Application 4

(For a two-floppy disk system, insert Help disk.) Press F1, select Keyboard Index, select Moving the Cell Pointer. Read the information about moving the cell pointer around your screen. Press Esc to return to the blank spreadsheet.

Application 5

Exit and reenter Lotus.

3

Creating a Spreadsheet

Spreadsheets, or worksheets, are commonly used in bookkeeping or accounting. However, any information that can be structured as rows and columns on a page can be set up as a spreadsheet.

A sample spreadsheet is shown in Figure 3-1. It details the expenses of a four-member family over four months. Each of the seven columns has a label at the top. The five rows contain text and values.

Preliminary Steps to Create a Spreadsheet

Before you begin creating your first spreadsheet, review the following steps to build a spreadsheet:

1. Display the blank spreadsheet.
2. Enter labels.
3. Enter values and formulas, as needed, into cells.
4. Enter the file name and save the file to disk.
5. Retrieve the file; make revisions.
6. Print the file.

In this chapter, you will learn how to display a blank spreadsheet, enter data into it, save it, and print it. As you learn to build a spreadsheet, we will offer additional helpful information to expand your knowledge of Lotus 1-2-3. For instance, we will tell you how to "copy" your keystrokes from one cell or group of cells (a range) to another area of the spreadsheet. Copying keystrokes saves keying time.

1990 EXPENSES JOHN HILL FAMILY

	Hse.Pmt	Util	Phone	Gasoline	Groceries	US Cr.Cd	Total
Jan	455	151	42	89	380	66	1183
Feb	455	148	39	92	410	66	1210
Mar	455	125	33	88	370	66	1137
Apr	455	90	37	89	390	66	1127
Total	1820	514	151	358	1550	264	4657

Figure 3-1 Sample spreadsheet.

Entering Data

To enter data in a cell, use the following steps:

1. Move the cell pointer to a cell.

2. Key the entry. As you key the entry, each character appears on the second line of the control panel, which is called the *entry line*. The cursor indicates the cell location where the next character you key will appear.

3. Complete either (a) or (b).

    a. Press any pointer-movement key to complete the entry and move the pointer to another cell.

    b. Press Enter to complete the cell entry and keep the pointer in that cell.

4. The entry disappears from the second line of the control panel and appears in the cell.

1-2-3 Menus

A menu is a list of commands from which you may make selections. There are two types of menus in 1-2-3: the Main Menu and the Submenu. The Main Menu appears on the second line of the control panel when you key the forward slash (/) key. The Submenu is displayed when you make a selection from the Main Menu; it shows all the tasks that may be selected for each highlighted Main Menu command. The mode indicator changes from READY to MENU when you key the slash (/). Figure 3-2 illustrates the two menus.

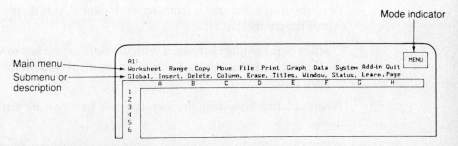

Figure 3-2   Main Menu and Submenu.

Command	Action
Worksheet	Lists commands that affect the entire worksheet
Range	Affects the worksheet but only within a specific range, such as erasing cells
Copy	Copies information from one cell or group of cells to another area of the worksheet
Move	Moves a row range, column range, or block to a new location
File	Saves, retrieves, lists, or erases files
Print	Writes all or part of the worksheet to the printer or onto a disk file
Graph	Specifies the graph type and the data to make up a graph when it is displayed
Data	Allows you to enter and analyze data in a worksheet
System	Lets you leave 1-2-3 temporarily, use a DOS command, and then return to 1-2-3
Add-in	Lets you add in programs created by Lotus and other software developers, which can run while using Lotus and provide additional capabilities; examples are Always and Macro Library programs
Quit	Ends your 1-2-3 session

Figure 3-3 Main Menu commands.

Figure 3-3 is a list of the Main Menu commands.

To view the menus, use the following steps:

1 Load 1-2-3 and insert your data disk in drive B (or drive A disk if using a hard drive system) if you have not already done so.

2 Key: / (the menus appear). The first highlighted word in the Main Menu is Worksheet. The Submenu (starting with Global...) is displayed on the third line of the control panel.

3 Practice highlighting each word with the right arrow key to view each menu; the highlighted commands' Submenus are displayed on the third line of the control panel.

4 When you finish viewing the menus, press Esc. You are returned to READY mode.

TIPS:
1. Pressing Esc allows you to leave any menu selection, one menu at a time, until you return to READY mode.
2. It is a little difficult to remember how each Main Menu command and its Submenu tasks work. To read a brief description about each one, use F1 (Help mode).

Erasing a Cell

Should you key text or enter data incorrectly, 1-2-3 allows you to erase or blank out information in a cell.

To practice entering data in and erasing a cell, use the following steps:

1. Press Home (to move the pointer to cell A1 if it isn't already there).

2. Key: your first name.

3. Press Enter (to complete the entry and keep the cell pointer in cell A1).

4. Key: / (to display the Main Menu).

5. Key: R (to accept Range). The Range Submenu appears in the control panel.

6. Key: E (to accept Erase) or highlight to move the pointer. The prompt—Enter range to erase: A1..A1—appears on the control panel.

7. Press Enter (to accept the range). The text should be erased.

TIP: Remember that you can press Esc to cancel an invalid cell or a selection for a command.

Types of Data

A cell may contain three types of data: labels, values, and formulas. When you key the first character of an entry, the READY mode indicator changes to either VALUE or LABEL, to show which type of data you are keying. When you complete an entry, the mode indicator changes back to READY.

Labels

Label entries are descriptive text. Label entries, such as January, Difference, and Percentage, are used to organize the numbers in columns and rows.

Labels have the following characteristics:

1. Labels can begin with a character that does not indicate the start of a value or a formula.

2. Labels can contain from 1 to 240 characters.

3. Labels can contain values, as long as the first character is not a value.

A label aligns on the left edge of a cell. You can change the alignment if you wish.

Values

Values are easy to enter in the worksheet. Values have the following characteristics:

1. Values must begin with one of 17 characters: the numbers 0 through 9, ., +, -, $, (, @, or #.

2. Values can contain from 1 to 240 characters.

3. Values cannot include spaces or commas.

4. Values can have no more than one decimal point.

A value aligns on the right edge of a cell. You cannot change the alignment of a value entry.

Formulas

Formulas explain how value entries are to be calculated. A formula results in a number or a numerical value.

Formulas have the following characteristics:

1. Formulas must begin with one of 17 characters: the numbers 0 through 9, ., +, -, $, (, @, or #.

2. Formulas can contain from 1 to 240 characters.

3. Formulas cannot contain spaces, except within a range name or a text string (see Chapter 4).

4. Formulas must begin with a + (plus sign) or parenthesis if the first part of the formula is a cell address.

After you enter the formula, its result, or value, appears in the cell. To view the formula itself, move the cell pointer to the cell that contains the formula and look at the first line of the control panel, the cell address line.

TIP: When you make a text entry that could be interpreted as a formula or value, you must specify that the entry is text by preceding it with an apostrophe ('). For example, the label for the year 1990 on the spreadsheet would be interpreted as a value (number). Therefore, type an apostrophe (') before it so that it will be treated as a label—'1990.

Correcting Mistakes

Use the following steps to correct mistakes before you press Enter:

1. Press Backspace.
2. Rekey the entry.
3. Press Enter or a pointer-movement key.

Use the following steps to correct mistakes after you press Enter:

1. Place the pointer in the cell containing the error.
2. Key the new entry.
3. Press Enter or a pointer-movement key.

Entering Labels

Spreadsheets are more easily understood when identified by a title (label). Sample titles include Income Statement, Balance Sheet, and Expenses.

To create a title for your spreadsheet, complete the following steps:

1. Place the cell pointer in cell A1. (Press Home if the pointer is not already there.)

2. Key : '1990 EXPENSES JOHN HILL FAMILY (all in caps, as shown here). Use the apostrophe (') before the entry so that 1-2-3 will know it is a label, not a value or formula.

3. Press Enter. Text will spill over into empty cells. That's okay.

Entering Column Labels

Now you're ready to enter column labels on your spreadsheet. To enter column labels, complete the following steps:

1. Move the cell pointer to cell A3, to leave a blank line (A2) under the heading.

2. Move the cell pointer to cell B3.

3. Key: Hse.Pmt

4. Press the right arrow.

5. Enter the remaining column labels:

   In C3, Key: Util   (Press right arrow.)
   In D3, Key: Phone   (Press right arrow.)

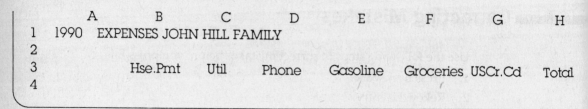

	A	B	C	D	E	F	G	H
1	1990	EXPENSES JOHN HILL FAMILY						
2								
3		Hse.Pmt	Util	Phone	Gasoline	Groceries	USCr.Cd	Total
4								

Figure 3-4   Title and column labels.

In E3, key: Gasoline	(Press right arrow.)
In F3, key: Groceries	(Press right arrow.)
In G3, key: USCr.Cd	(Press right arrow.)
In H3, key: Total	(Press Enter)

Compare your screen with Figure 3-4.

Changing the Column Width

Notice that the column labels aren't evenly spaced within a cell. See how the column label Groceries runs into the label USCr.Cd. You need to make an adjustment to widen the columns; then you must align all labels to the right margin of the cells.

To widen all columns, use the following steps:

1. Press Home. You should be able to view your spreadsheet from this position.

2. Key: / (to view the Main Menu).

3. Key: W (for *Worksheet*).

4. Key: G (for *Global*—meaning all columns).

5. Key: C (for *Column* width—since you want to widen your columns). Do not press Enter. Notice that 9 appears on the entry line. That's because the default column width is 9 characters.

6. Key: 11 (The column width increases to 11 characters on the entry line.) Press Enter (to execute the command).

Aligning Labels

Lotus 1-2-3 automatically aligns label entries with the left margin of a cell and aligns value entries with the right margin of a cell. You can change the alignment of a range of label entries by using the /Range Label command. Your options are left, right, and center.

To align the labels with the values, complete the following steps:

1 Move the pointer to cell B3.

2 Key: / (to view the Main Menu).

3 Key: R (for *Range*).

4 Key: L (for *Label*).

5 Key: R (for *Right*).

6 Notice that the mode indicator displays POINT. Key: . (period) to anchor the pointer.

7 Use the right arrow key to highlight the range B3 through H3.

8 Press Enter.

Watch your screen. All the column labels move to the right margin of each cell. In this position, they will match the alignment of the values in each column.

Whenever possible, plan to enter consecutive labels or values. For this reason, column A labels will be entered as a vertical group; then the values will be entered as a vertical group in column B.

To enter the data in the cells, use the following steps:

1 Press Home. Move the pointer to cell A5.

2 Key: Jan (the first entry in the cell).

3 Press the down arrow. Notice that the pointer moves down to cell A6.

4 Continue to key each month (as shown in Figure 3-5), pressing the down arrow after each entry.

5 In cell A10, key: Total. (Press Enter.)

6 Position the pointer in cell B5.

Compare your screen with Figure 3-5.

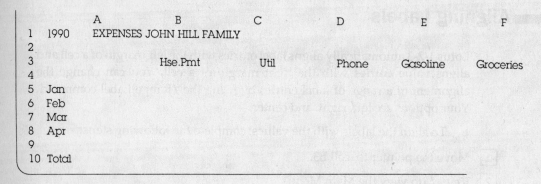

	A	B	C	D	E	F
1	1990	EXPENSES JOHN HILL FAMILY				
2						
3		Hse.Pmt	Util	Phone	Gasoline	Groceries
4						
5	Jan					
6	Feb					
7	Mar					
8	Apr					
9						
10	Total					

Figure 3-5 Data entered in column A.

Entering Values

You are now ready to enter the first numerical data in your spreadsheet. You may enter values with the number keys at the top of your keyboard or you may use the shift key with the numeric keypad.

1 Move the pointer to B5.

2 With your left hand, hold down the left Shift Key (keep it down) and key: 455, using the numeric keypad. Key the figure as a whole number without a $ (dollar sign). Release the Shift Key.

3 Press the down arrow to enter the amount in cell B5.

4 Key the amount for each remaining house payment, using the left Shift and the numeric keypad. Press the down arrow after each entry (see Figure 3-6).

5 Move to cell C5.

6 Key the amount for each utility bill (see Figure 3-6). Press the down arrow after each entry.

7 Move to cell D5.

8 Continue keying the other expenses.

9 Move to cell H5.

TIP: Always verify your data when you finish keying.

Entering Formulas

There are several methods available in 1-2-3 for entering formulas. An efficient method to use for adding is the @sum function. The @sum function is best used to add long columns of data. This function also illustrates 1-2-3's ability

B		C	D	E	F	G	H
Hse.Pmt		Util	Phone	Gasoline	Groceries	US Cr.Cd	Total
455		151	42	89	380	66	
455		148	39	92	410	66	
455		125	33	88	370	66	
455		90	37	89	390	66	

Figure 3-6 Data entered in columns B through G.

to manually point to a data cell in order to enter that particular cell into a formula. The @sum function introduces the concept of a range.

To use the @sum function, follow the steps below. Watch carefully what happens on your screen.

1. The cell pointer should be at H5.

2. Key: @sum([This opening parenthesis starts the formula.]

3. Use the left arrow to position the pointer at cell B5. Do not use F5 (GoTo) to go to cell B5.

4. Key: . (This period marks, or anchors, the beginning of the range. Notice that the period appears twice in the entry line.)

5. Use the right arrow to position the pointer at cell G5, which is the last cell to be added. Do not use F5 (GoTo) to go to cell G5.

6. Key:) [This closing parenthesis completes the sum formula.]

7. Press the down arrow. The @sum function produces the value 1183 in cell H5, and the pointer is positioned at cell H6.

8. Continue using the @sum function for the remaining rows.

Compare your screen with Figure 3-7.

C	D	E	F	G	H
Util	Phone	Gasoline	Groceries	US Cr.Cd	Total
151	42	89	380	66	1183
148	39	92	410	66	1210
125	33	88	370	66	1137
90	37	89	390	66	1127

Figure 3-7 Column H totals.

Copying Formulas

In the previous exercise, you entered the formula for calculating each month's total (in column H) four different times. Now you will learn a shortcut for entering the same formula several times simultaneously. Lotus 1-2-3's Copy feature can duplicate cell descriptions in other cell positions. Copying a formula to the other cells in a column can save a considerable amount of time and can eliminate keying errors. The Copy function has many features; however, in this text, you will simply copy the formula from one cell to other cells.

You are now ready to obtain a total for the various expenses. But, instead of repeatedly keying the formula into each cell, as you did in cells H5 through H8, you are going to instruct 1-2-3 to copy it to an entire range of cells.

To enter the formula, use the following steps:

1. Press Home. Move the pointer to cell B10.
2. Key: @sum([The opening parenthesis starts the formula.]
3. Manually move the cell pointer up to cell B5.
4. Key: . (This period anchors the pointer.)
5. Manually move the cell pointer down to cell B8.
6. Key:) [The closing parenthesis ends the formula.]
7. Press Enter (to execute the command). The value 1820 should be displayed in cell B10.

To copy the formula, complete the following steps. (The pointer should be in cell B10. Move it there if it isn't.)

1. Key: / (to display the Main Menu).
2. Key: C (for *Copy*).
3. Press Enter (to specify Range to Copy FROM: B10).
4. Move the cell pointer to cell C10 (to indicate the starting cell of Range to Copy TO:).
5. Key: . (to tell 1-2-3 that you are anchoring the pointer).
6. Move the cell pointer to H10, which is the last cell in the range to receive a copy of the formula. Cells C10 through H10 should be highlighted.

Hse.Pmt	Util	Phone	Gasoline	Groceries	US Cr.Cd	Total
455	151	42	89	380	66	1183
455	148	39	92	410	66	1210
455	125	33	88	370	66	1137
455	90	37	89	390	66	1127
1820	514	151	358	1550	264	4657

Figure 3-8 All data entered and totals calculated.

7 Press Enter. The formula should be copied into each of the specified cells. The value for the cells should also be calculated.

8 Your screen should look something like Figure 3-8. Move your cell pointer to each column total and view the formulas on the status line.

Saving a File

The spreadsheet on your screen exists only in the computer's random access memory (RAM). This memory is temporary. In other words, if you turn the computer off while the spreadsheet is on your screen, everything in this temporary memory will be lost.

Lotus 1-2-3's Save function copies data from the computer's RAM onto a data disk.

TIP: Save your spreadsheet frequently. In an accidental power failure, you lose only those entries that you made since the last time you saved your spreadsheet.

The computer sees your spreadsheet as a file, like a file in a file drawer. Now that you have completed the spreadsheet, you must give it a name and file (save) it. The diskette will be your file drawer. The process of saving the spreadsheet is actually the computer's writing it onto a disk.

Changing the Default Directory

Before naming and saving your file, change the default directory to B or A if using a hard drive. Changing the default directory will eliminate the extra keystrokes involved in entering "b:" each time you save or retrieve a file. The directory should be changed to the directory where you are saving your work as soon as Lotus is loaded each time.

Complete these steps to change the default directory to B (or A if using a hard drive system):

1. Insert your data disk in drive B and key: / F (for *File*) D (for *Directory*).
2. Key: b: (or a: if using a hard drive).
3. Press Enter.

To save the spreadsheet, use the following steps:

1. Key: / (to display the Main Menu) F (for File) S (for *Save*).
2. Key : 1990EXPS (without spacing or punctuation). You may use a combination of only 8 characters (letters and/or numbers) to name your file. Lotus 1-2-3 will add an extension .WK1 to the end of your file.
3. Press Enter. Wait. When the mode indicator changes back to READY, the file is saved.

Printing a Spreadsheet

The default page width is 72 characters, and the default page length is 66 lines. If your spreadsheet exceeds the page width, 1-2-3 prints as many columns as it can on the first page, then prints the remaining columns separately. Your spreadsheet will print on two pages. Printing on a separate page is not efficient, so you will learn how to condense the printing.

To print your spreadsheet, use the following steps:

1. Be certain the printer is ready.
2. Key: / (to display the Main Menu).
3. Key: P (for *Print*).
4. Key: P (for *Printer*, to send the spreadsheet to your printer).
5. Key: O (for *Options*).

6 Select Set up from the Options submenu.

7 Key: \015 (Press Enter).

8 Key: M (for Margins).

9 Key: R (for Right).

10 Key: 132 (for right margin). Quit the menu.

11 Key: R (for *Range*, to specify the range).

12 Move the cell pointer until it is positioned on cell A1. Key a period. Move the cell pointer to cell H10. Cells A1 through H10 should be highlighted. Press Enter (to accept the range).

13 Key: G (for *Go*, to tell the printer to begin printing).

14 When printing stops, key: P (for *Page*) to eject the printed sheet out of the printer. Lotus will print as much of your worksheet on one page as possible, then continue printing on a second page.

15 Key: Q (for *Quit*). This command leaves the Print Menu and returns you to READY mode.

1990 EXPENSES JOHN HILL FAMILY

	Hse.Pmt	Util	Phone	Gasoline	Groceries	US Cr.Cd	Total
Jan	455	151	42	89	380	66	1183
Feb	455	148	39	92	410	66	1210
Mar	455	125	33	88	370	66	1137
Apr	455	90	37	89	390	66	1127
Total	1820	514	151	358	1550	264	4657

Figure 3-9 Printed spreadsheet.

Your printed copy should print columns A through H on one page. Figure 3-9 shows the completed spreadsheet.

TIP: A faster way to highlight the range is to press Home, key a period, press End, and press Home again.

Canceling Printing

Suppose, after you begin printing, that you realize a change needs to be made on your spreadsheet, or you just want to stop the printer and cancel the print job. Lotus 1-2-3 provides a Cancel command for that purpose.

To cancel a print job, use the following step:

[1] Begin printing the file 1990EXPS, which you just printed. At the same time, press Ctrl and Break. The printer will stop. Some printers may continue to print a few more lines before stopping.

Erasing the Screen

After a spreadsheet is saved and printed, it still appears on your screen and in the computer's memory. The Erase command erases all the contents of the spreadsheet from the screen and from the computer's memory. For this reason, always save your spreadsheet before you erase it. A blank screen is provided to continue work.

To clear the screen, use the following steps:

[1] Press Esc until you are in READY mode.

[2] Key: / (to display the Main Menu).

[3] Key: W (for *Worksheet*).

[4] Key: E (for *Erase*). Notice that 1-2-3 asks on the prompt line: No you do not want to clear the screen or Yes you do want to clear the screen? (Be certain that you have saved the file before answering Yes.)

[5] Key: Y (for *Yes*). A blank worksheet is shown on your screen.

[6] Quit Lotus (/ Quit, Yes, Exit).

TIP: | To recover the spreadsheet to your screen, press Alt and F4 (UnDo command).

Summary

To build a spreadsheet:

1. Display the blank spreadsheet.
2. Enter labels.
3. Enter values and formulas, as needed, into cells.
4. Enter file name and save the file to the disk.
5. Retrieve the file; make revisions and save the file to disk.
6. Print the file.

To enter data in a cell:

1. Move the cell pointer to a cell.
2. Key the entry. As you key the entry, each character appears on the second line of the control panel. The cursor indicates where the next character you key will appear.
3. Complete either (a) or (b).

   a. Press any pointer-movement key to complete the entry and move the pointer to another cell.

   b. Press Enter to complete the cell entry and keep the pointer in that cell.
4. The entry disappears from the second line of the control panel and appears in the cell.

To view a menu:

1. Key: / (the menus appear). The first highlighted word in the Main Menu is Worksheet. The Submenu is displayed on the third line of the control panel.
2. When you finish viewing the menus, press Esc until you are returned to READY mode.

To erase a cell:

1. Place pointer on cell to be erased.
2. Key: / (to display the Main Menu).
3. Key: R (to accept Range).
4. Key: E (to accept Erase). A prompt—Enter range to erase: —appears on the control panel.
5. Press Enter (to accept the range). The text should be erased.

To widen all columns:

1. Press Home. You should be able to view your worksheet from this position.
2. Key: / (to view the Main Menu).
3. Key: W (for *Worksheet*).
4. Key: G (for *Global,* — meaning all columns).
5. Key: C (for *Column width,* — since you want to widen your columns). Do not press Enter. Notice that 9 appears on the entry line, because the default column width is 9 characters.
6. Key the desired column-width number on the entry line.
7. Press Enter (to execute the command).

To align labels:

1. Move the pointer to the cell.
2. Key: / (to view the Main Menu).
3. Key: R (for *Range*).
4. Key: L (for *Label*).
5. Key: R (for *Right*), L (for *Left*), or C (for *Center*).
6. Notice that the mode indicator displays POINT. Key: . (period) to anchor the pointer.
7. Use the arrow key to highlight desired cells.
8. Press Enter.

To copy a formula:

1. Move the pointer to the cell containing the formula.
2. Key: / (to display the Main Menu).
3. Key: C (for *Copy*).
4. Press Enter (to specify Range to Copy FROM:).
5. Move the cell pointer to a cell, to indicate the starting cell of Range to Copy TO:.
6. Key: . (to tell 1-2-3 that you are anchoring the pointer).
7. Move the cell pointer to the last cell in the range to receive a copy of the formula.
8. Press Enter. The formula should be copied into each of the specified cells. The value for the cells should also be calculated.

To change the default directory:

1. Insert your data disk and key: / F (for *File*) D (for *Directory*).
2. Key the desired drive and a colon.

To save a spreadsheet:

1. Key: / (to display the Main Menu) F (for *File*) S (for *Save*)
2. Key file name. Press Enter. Wait. When the mode indicator changes back to READY, the file is saved.

To print your spreadsheet:

1. Be certain the printer is ready.
2. Key: / (to display the Main Menu).
3. Key: P (for *Print*).
4. Key: P (for *Printer*, to send the worksheet to your printer).
5. Key: O (for *Options*).
6. Select Setup from the Options submenu.
7. Key: \015 (Press Enter)
8. Key: 132 (for right margin). Quit the menu.
9. Key: R (for *Range*, to specify the range).
10. Specify the range. Press Enter (to accept the range).
11. Key: G (for *Go*, to tell the printer to begin printing).
12. Key: P (for *Page*, to eject the printed sheet from the printer).
13. Key: Q (for *Quit*). This command leaves the Print Menu and returns you to READY mode.

To erase the screen:

1. Press Esc until you are in READY mode.
2. Key: / (to display the Main Menu).
3. Key: W (for *Worksheet*).
4. Key: E (for *Erase*). Notice that 1-2-3 asks on the prompt line: Yes you want to clear the screen or No you do not want to clear the screen?
5. Key: Y (for *Yes*).

To UnDo your last action:

1. Press Alt and F4.

Applications

Where appropriate, enter a formula; then use the Copy command to copy formulas needed in other columns. Widen the columns where necessary. Align all labels to the right.

Application 1

Create the following sales summary as a spreadsheet. Enter the formulas to total each department. Save the file, name it SUMMARY, and print one copy.

GASTON DEPARTMENT STORE
Sales Summary, March 31, 19--

	Department A	Department B	Department C
	1223.14	2112.99	3221.66
	1544.50	7659.88	3445.29
	3981.10	1256.44	2333.90
	2421.30	4578.25	5921.40
	5322.80	3452.60	1900.78
Total			

Application 2

Create the following spreadsheet. Enter the formulas to total each column. Save the file, name it HOLLOW, and print one copy.

OAK HOLLOW HOMEOWNERS' ASSOCIATION
Association Dues, 19--

Homeowner	Amount Due	Amount Paid	Balance Due
Johnson	30		30
Barrett	22	15	7
Smith	15	15	
Reynolds	50	25	25
Green	17	17	
Total			

Application 3

Create the following spreadsheet. Enter the formula to calculate the total. Save the file, name it DPE, and print one copy.

DELTA PI EPSILON
19-- State Conference

City	Attendance
Abilene	8
Brownwood	2
Carthage	3
Dallas	15
Fort Worth	18
Houston	25
Tyler	4
Total	

Application 4

Create the following spreadsheet. Enter the formula to total the sales. Save the file, name it SOFTWARE, and print one copy.

DISCOUNT SOFTWARE WORLD
Software Sales, July, 19--

Software	No. Sales
WordPerfect	1231
WordStar	1008
Microsoft Word	1743
MultiMate Advantage	1899
DisplayWrite	7764
Total	

Application 5

Create the following partial income statement as a spreadsheet. Enter the formulas to total the columns. Save the file, name it DELANEY, and compress-print one copy. Be sure to change back to regular-size print.

DELANEY CORPORATION
Income Statement
For Six Months Ending June 30, 19--

Revenue:
Professional Fees	75000
Interest Income	9500
Total Revenue	

Expenses:
Rent Expense	6000
Utilities Expense	1500
Phone Expense	500
Repair Expense	2500
Wages Expense	12000
Total Expenses	

4

Editing a Spreadsheet

After completing a spreadsheet, it is often helpful to make changes to update information. In this chapter, we will discuss file lists; editing data; displaying formulas; inserting, deleting, and moving data; and other helpful 1-2-3 editing functions.

File List

1-2-3 has a file directory called a File List. The directory lists all the file names of a particular type saved in the current directory. (The file name consists of a name ending with an extension formed by a period and two or three identifying letters.) For example, Worksheet lists all .WK files. Print displays all .PRN files, and Graph displays .PIC files. Other displays all files in the current directory. Figure 4-1 is a sample File List of spreadsheet names. Remember that the computer sees each spreadsheet as a file.

TIP: | If you haven't already changed the default directory from A to B, (or from C to A if using a hard drive system) do so now by following these steps:

1. Insert your data disk and key: /F (for File) D (for Directory).

2. Key: b: (or key: a:)

3. Press Enter.

Remember that you have to change the default directory each time you boot your system and load Lotus 1-2-3.

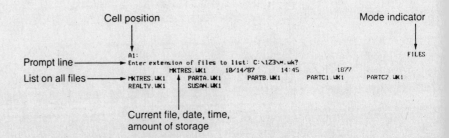

Figure 4-1 Example of File List.

To view a File List on your data disk, complete the following steps:

1. Be certain your data disk is in drive B (or drive A for hard disk users).

2. Key: /F (for *File*).

3. Key: L (for *List*).

4. Key: W (for *Worksheet*, to view all the worksheet files in the current directory).

5. Press Enter to return to READY mode.

TIPS:
1. To change the current directory for future sessions, use / Worksheet Global Default Directory followed by / Worksheet Global Default Update.
2. Use the File List command after you erase a file, to be certain that it is erased from the list of current files.

Retrieving a File

Once a file has been saved on disk, you can retrieve it very easily.

To retrieve a file you have saved on your data disk, use the following steps:

1. Your data disk should be positioned in drive B, with drive B as the default directory. For hard drive users, use drive A.

2. From READY mode, key: / (to display the Main Menu).

3. Key: F (for *File*).

4. Key: R (for *Retrieve*). A list of file names of existing spreadsheet files appears. The file name 1990EXPS, which you created earlier, appears on the third line of the control panel. The file name extension .WK1 is automatically added by 1-2-3.

TIP: To select a file, move the menu pointer to the file name you want. Press Enter.

5. The file named 1990EXPS.WK1 is highlighted. Press Enter. The spreadsheet you created in Chapter 3 should appear.

Entering Additional Text

In this chapter, you will enter additional data onto your spreadsheet. These data are highlighted in Figure 4-2.

To add more text to a spreadsheet, simply move your pointer to the cell where you want the text to begin and enter it.

1990 EXPENSES JOHN HILL FAMILY				1182 Hill Street, Dallas, TX 75222			
	Hse.Pmt	Util	Phone	Gasoline	Food	US Cr.Cd	Total
January	455	151	42	89	380	66	1183
February	455	148	39	92	410	66	1210
March	455	125	33	88	370	66	1137
April	455	90	37	89	390	66	1127
May							
Total	1820	514	151	358	1550	264	4657
% of Total	0.390809534	0.1103714838	0.0324243075	0.0768735237	0.3328322955	0.0566888555	1

Figure 4-2 Additional data to enter onto worksheet.

Add the following text to the file named 1990EXPS by completing these steps:

1 Move your pointer to cell D1 and key: '1182 Hill Street, Dallas, TX 75222 (start with an apostrophe; the text will spill over into the following cells).

2 Press Enter.

To increase the width of the columns, complete the following steps:

1 Key: / W (for *Worksheet*).

2 Key: G (for *Global*).

3 Key: C (for *Column width*).

4 Key: 14 (to replace the previous width).

5 Press Enter.

To add additional text to your spreadsheet, use the following steps:

1 Move the cell pointer to cell A9. Key: May.

2 Press the down arrow. The totals should be on row 10.

3 Move the pointer to cell A12 and key: % of Total.

4 Press Enter.

TIP: You have set up the spreadsheet for the month of May. However, you will not be entering any amounts for this month. In the beginning, when you plan a spreadsheet like that in our example, enter 12 months. At the end of each month, all you will have to do is enter each type of expense, rather than set up each month.

Using EDIT Mode

The F2 key is used to display EDIT mode. When using F2, turn off Insert by pressing Ins. The status indicator OVR (meaning Overstrike) is displayed.

You have edited data on the entry line before sending it to a cell by backspacing, and you have deleted data from a cell by erasing the cell. Lotus 1-2-3 provides an easy way to edit data already in a cell—by using the Delete (Del) key, located at the lower-right corner of your keyboard.

To practice using the Del key to edit data already in a cell, follow these steps:

1. Place your pointer in the cell to be edited. Move to cell F3.

2. Suppose you want to change Groceries to Food. Press F2 (Edit). Lotus 1-2-3 brings the entry in cell F3 to the entry line. Notice that you are now in EDIT mode.

3. Press Home to move the pointer to the beginning of the entry line.

4. Press Del 10 times to delete "Groceries.

5. Key: "Food (the next column label). Typing the double quote before the label Food aligns the new column label to the right.

6. Press Enter. The new entry replaces the column label in cell F3.

To practice inserting new text into data already in a cell, follow these steps:

1. Move the pointer to the cell to be edited. Press Home and move to cell A5. (Pressing Home and moving to the cell allows you to see more lines in the spreadsheet. Pressing F5 [GoTo] to move the cell pointer does not display as many lines.)

2. Press F2 (Edit). Again, 1-2-3 brings the entry in cell A5 to the entry line and changes to EDIT mode.

3. Notice that the pointer is one space after the *n* in Jan. Key: uary (to spell January in full).

4. Press the down arrow.

	1990 EXPENSES JOHN HILL FAMILY			1182 Hill Street, Dallas, TX 75222			
1							
2							
3	Hse.Pmt	Util	Phone	Gasoline	Food	US Cr.Cd	Total
4							
5	January	455	151	42	89	380	66	1183
6	February	455	148	39	92	410	66	1210
7	March	455	125	33	88	370	66	1137
8	April	455	90	37	89	390	66	1127
9	May						
10	Total	1820	514	151	358	1550	264	4657
11							
12	% of Total						
13							
14							
15							
16							
17							
18							
19							
20							

Figure 4-3 Edited worksheet.

5 Edit the rest of the months by spelling each month in full. After keying a month, press the down arrow and repeat steps 2 through 4 above.

Your screen should look like Figure 4-3.

Calculating Percentages

When you copied the formulas for totaling columns across and down the spreadsheet, 1-2-3 automatically changed the column or row address to the adjacent column or row. For example, 1-2-3 adjusted the formula @sum(B5.G5) in cell B10 to read @sum(B6.G6) when it copied the formula into cell C10. In this way, the formula specified a new range each time you copied it.

Your screen now displays the results of those calculations. How can these totals be used to determine a percentage of the total expenses for each category? The desired formula can be stated simply: What percentage of the total expenses is our house payment to date? When we insert the information from the cells that contain the figures from our spreadsheet, we could restate the formula to read: What % of H10 is B10? B10 divided by H10 will give you the percentage.

Lotus 1-2-3 has identified certain symbols on the keyboard as representing specific math functions. For instance, the slash (/) means divide. Therefore, our formula would now read +B10/H10 (or 1820 divided by 4657). The formula for Utilities would be +C10/H10.

The formula required to compute each percentage presents a special problem. We want to copy our basic formula to compute each category's percentage of the total. However, we do not want cell H10 to automatically adjust to cell I10, then to cell J10, and so on, as the formula is repeatedly copied. 1-2-3 uses dollar signs ($) to hold cell H10 constant, so that it will not change when the formula is copied. Our basic formula in cell B12 would be entered as +B10/$H$10. When this formula is copied into cell C10, it will appear as +C10/$H$10. In this manner, the total of each column will be divided by the total in cell H10.

To enter the formula for computing percentages, follow these steps:

1. Move the pointer to B12.

2. Key: +B10/$H$10 (Enter the plus symbol before B10 so that 1-2-3 will recognize this entry as a formula rather than a label. Remember that the two $ serve to hold cell H10 constant when the formula is copied.)

3. Press Enter. (.390809534 appears in B12, which represents 39%.)

4. Copy the formula in B12 to cells C12.H12 to compute the percentage for each column. Refer to page 42 for a review of copying formulas.

5. Save your file. Key: / F S (*File Save*); press Enter to accept the file name; select R (for *Replace*).

Choosing Replace means that you will "save over" the existing file of the same name with the data from the current spreadsheet. Choosing Cancel means that you will return to the current spreadsheet in the READY mode, and nothing is saved. Selecting Backup copies the spreadsheet file on disk to a backup file with the same file name but the extension .BAK and saves the current spreadsheet with the existing file name and the extension .WK1.

6. Print your file. Key: / P P R (for *Print Printer Range*); specify to print the range A1.H12; Enter; Go.

7. Key: P (*Page*) to eject the paper from the printer.

1990 EXPENSES JOHN HILL FAMILY   1182 Hill Street, Dallas, TX 75222

	Hse.Pmt	Util	Phone	Gasoline	Food	US Cr.Cd	Total
January	455	151	42	89	380	66	1183
February	455	148	39	92	410	66	1210
March	455	125	33	88	370	66	1137
April	455	90	37	89	390	66	1127
May							
Total	1820	514	151	358	1550	264	4657
% of Total	0.390809534	0.1103714838	0.0324243075	0.0768735237	0.3328322955	0.0566888555	1

Figure 4-4 Percents calculated and displayed on worksheet.

8 Key: Q (*Quit*) to leave the Print menu.

Your copy should look something like Figure 4-4.

To make the decimal results in row 12 more readable, let's change the format from decimals to percentages. By selecting the Percent Format, you will be able to display percentages with a specific number of decimal places.

To display percentages, use the following steps:

1 Key: / (to display the Main Menu).

2 Key: R (for *Range*).

3 Key: F (for *Format*).

4 Key: P (for *Percent*).

5 To select two decimal places, press Enter.

6 To specify the range, key: B12.H12

7 Press Enter.

Your spreadsheet should show the following percentages:

Hse.Pmt = 39.08%
Util = 11.04%
Phone = 3.24%
Gasoline = 7.69%
Food = 33.28%
USCr.Cd = 5.67%
Total = 100.00%

8 To save the worksheet on your data disk, key: / F S (for *File Save*).

9 The file name appears as 1990EXPS.WK1.

10 Press Enter to accept the file name.

11 Select R (for *Replace*).

Displaying Formulas with the Global Command

You have entered several formulas in your spreadsheet. Lotus 1-2-3 displayed each total or percentage in the proper cell.

Until now, to see which formula was entered in any one cell, you would view the formula at the cell address line by moving the pointer from cell to cell and reading the formulas one at a time. When working with formulas, it is often helpful to view them all at once. Lotus 1-2-3 provides a Global command that allows you to do this. When you use the command, the formulas temporarily replace the results of the formulas' calculations except when the formula's format has been changed. When you repeat the command, the results reappear.

To display formulas with the Global command, use the following steps:

1 Go Home.

2 Key: / (to display the Main Menu).

3 Key: W (for *Worksheet*).

4 Key: G (for *Global*).

5 Key: F (for *Format*).

1990 EXPENSES JOHN HILL FAMILY   1182 Hill Street, Dallas, TX 75222

	Hse.Pmt	Food	Util	Phone	Gasoline	US Cr.Cd	Total
January	455	380	151	42	89	66	@SUM(B5..G5)
February	455	410	148	39	92	66	@SUM(B6..G6)
March	455	370	125	33	88	66	@SUM(B7..G7)
April	455	390	90	37	89	66	@SUM(B8..G8)
May							
Total	@SUM(B5..B8)	@SUM(C5..C8)	@SUM(D5..D8)	@SUM(E5..E8)	@SUMF5..F8)	@SUM(G5..G8)	@SUM(H5..H8)
% of Total	39.08%	33.28%	11.04%	3.24%	7.69%	5.67%	100.00%

Figure 4-5   Formulas displayed on worksheet.

6   Key: T (for *Text*). The formulas you entered are displayed in row 10. The formulas affected by the format change are not displayed. Your screen should look like Figure 4-5.

7   Key: / W G F G (for *Worksheet Global Format General*) to clear the screen of the formulas.

8   Key: / W E Y (for *Worksheet Erase Yes*) to erase the worksheet from your screen.

1-2-3 Formulas

Rather than do arithmetic calculations manually, you can use 1-2-3 formulas to perform calculations automatically within a range of cells. You have already used the addition and division operations in your spreadsheet. Figure 4-6 describes 1-2-3's arithmetic functions.

To view formulas from a previously stored worksheet, use the following steps:

1   Be certain that a blank spreadsheet is displayed on your screen and that the default directory is B (or A for a hard disk).

2   Retrieve the file named TRAVEL from your data disk (/ F R).

3   Go to cell D5 to view how the subtraction operation was used in column D (*Difference*): +C5-B5.

Arithmetic Function	Keyboard Symbol	1-2-3 Formula	Explanation
Addition	+	@sum or +F3+F4	Add contents of range of cells (F3,F4)
Subtraction	-	+E15-F17	Subtract value of cell F17 from value of cell E15
Multiplication	*	+G5*H5	Multiply value of cell G5 by value of cell H5
Division	/	+G10/F13	Divide value of cell G10 by value of cell F13
	@avg	@avg(G10.F13)	Add value of cell G10 to value of cell F13 and divide by 2

Figure 4-6 Arithmetic functions.

4 To display the formulas, using the Global command, key: / W G F T (for *Worksheet Global Format Text*).

5 To clear the formulas from the screen, key: / W G F G (for *Worksheet Global Format General*).

6 To erase this spreadsheet from the screen, key: / W E Y (for *Worksheet Erase Yes*). Remember that this command erases the file from the computer's memory, not from your data disk because the file was previously saved.

Inserting Columns and Rows

After you have created a spreadsheet, you may want to change the original spreadsheet. For example, you may want to add or delete a formula, row, or column to make the spreadsheet more meaningful and useful. After you have made the revisions, you must save the spreadsheet on the disk, replacing the old one; otherwise, the revisions will not be permanent. Lotus 1-2-3's commands allow you to enter columns and rows with the Insert command or to remove them with the Delete command.

Columns and rows can be inserted using 1-2-3's Worksheet Insert command (/ W I). When you insert rows and columns, the existing rows and columns move to make room for the new ones. Lotus 1-2-3 adjusts any formulas so that they continue to refer to the same data.

To insert a column, use the following steps:

1. Retrieve the worksheet file named 1990EXPS.

2. Position your cell pointer at the cell where you want to add the new column: cell E3.

3. Key: / (to display the Main Menu).

4. Key: W (for *Worksheet*).

5. Key: I (for *Insert*, to insert a column between D and E).

6. To select a column, key: C (for *Column*).

7. Specify the range or highlight the number of columns you want to insert. E3.E3 will appear because your pointer is there.

8. Press Enter. A new blank column appears, and the data in columns E and F are automatically moved to the right of the new blank column. You have added a new column between D and F.

Deleting Columns and Rows

You may want to delete a row or column when it is no longer useful or when current data should replace old data. Deleting is quite simple and basically the same as inserting a row or column.

To delete a column, use the following steps:

1. Be certain that the cell pointer is in cell E3.

2. Key: / (to display the Main Menu).

3. Key: W (for *Worksheet*).

4. Key: D (for *Delete*).

5. Key: C (for *Column*).

6. Specify the range if you want to delete more than one column. E3.E3 will appear because your cell pointer is there.

7. Press Enter. The column has been deleted.

All columns to the right of a deleted column shift to the left, and all rows below a deleted row move up.

TIP: If a formula in a deleted column depends on a previous value, the message ERR (Error) will be displayed. Rekey the value and check its correctness before continuing with your spreadsheet. Deleting rows and columns requires careful attention to the effect of the deletions on the spreadsheet values.

Moving Data

The Move command transfers a range of cell entries from one location in the spreadsheet to another. This powerful command allows you to redesign your spreadsheet without having to rekey information.

TIP: If you want to move a range of cells, be sure to insert a new column or row for it first. If you don't make room for the data, they will replace the current information in the column or row to which you are moving the data.

As a practice exercise, move Food to column C, using the following steps:

1. To insert a column at cell C3, position the pointer in C3 and key: / W I C (for *Worksheet Insert Column*). Press Enter to accept the range. This step is important, because it ensures that you will not lose the data in the existing column.

2. Key: / (to display the Main Menu).

3. Key: M (for *Move*). The prompt reads: Enter range to move FROM:

4. Specify the FROM range.

5. Key: G3.G12

6. Press Enter. The prompt reads: Enter range to move TO:

7. C3 already appears. Press Enter to select C3. The formulas are adjusted to their new locations.

8. Move the cell pointer to cell G3.

9. To delete column G, key: / W D C (for *Worksheet Delete Column*). Press Enter to accept the range.

10. Save the spreadsheet on your data disk; key: / F S. Press Enter to accept file name. Key: R (*Replace*). Remember that Replace erases the old file on your data disk and replaces it with the revised one. Cancel returns you to READY mode, where you choose a new file name for the spreadsheet you want to save.

11. To erase the spreadsheet from the screen, key: / W E Y (for *Worksheet Erase Yes*).

Formatting a Spreadsheet

Earlier in this chapter, you used a Format command when you expanded the column width to 14 characters and again when you right-justified the column titles in row 3. Several other Format commands are often used.

The **Justification** command left-justifies text and right-justifies numbers. These are the default format values when you begin a new spreadsheet.

The **Hide** option keeps certain information confidential. This command allows you to specify cells you do not want displayed or printed. To hide an entire column, key: / *Worksheet Column Hide*. To redisplay a hidden column, key: / *Worksheet Column Display*. To hide a range, key: / *Range Format Hidden*. To redisplay a hidden range, key: / *Range Format Reset*.

The **Integer Display Format** displays all values rounded to the nearest whole number. You key: / *Range Format Global Fixed* (with 0 decimal places). Then you press Enter.

To view the format options, use the following steps:

1 Key: / (to display the Main Menu).

2 Key: W (for *Worksheet*).

3 Key: G (for *Global*).

4 Key: F (for *Format*). Using the right arrow, highlight the various options and read about each one in MENU mode on the Help line.

5 Press Esc four times to return to READY mode.

Review Basic Spreadsheet Steps

Now that you have created, revised, and printed a spreadsheet, take time to review the basic steps used on spreadsheets.

1. Set up the format.

    a. Worksheet Global Column width (/ W G C) sets the column width for all columns.

    b. Worksheet Global Format (/ W G F) sets the data format for all cells.

    c. Make worksheet column adjustments. / Worksheet Column (/ W C Set width) adjusts the column width for specific columns. (/ R F) sets the data format for a specific range.

    d.   Set up Range(s).

2.   Complete the spreadsheet.

    a.   Enter column labels.

    b.   Enter row labels (text).

    c.   Enter formulas.

    d.   Enter data.

3.   Save the file.

    a.   File Save (/ F S) saves the completed spreadsheet on the disk. Replace saves the changed spreadsheet to disk.

4.   Print the file.

    a.   Print Printer Options Range Go (/ P P O R G) prints the spreadsheet. Page (P) advances paper from printer. Quit exits Print menu.

5.   W E Yes erases the file from the screen.

6.   Quit Yes (/ Q Y) returns you to DOS.

Summary

To change the default drive:

  1. Key: / F (for *File*).

  2. Key: D (for *Directory*).

  3. Key: b:

  4. Press Enter.

To view a File List.

  1. Key: / F (for *File*).

  2. Key: L (for *List*).

  3. Select *Worksheet, Print, Graph,* or *Other*.

  4. Press Enter to return to READY mode.

To retrieve a file:

  1. From READY mode, key: / (to display the Main Menu).

  2. Key: F (for *File*).

  3. Key: R (for *Retrieve*). Name of file to retrieve (A:/) appears.

  4. Backspace to erase previous drive. Key: b: (unless drive has already been changed).

5. Key file name.

6. Press Enter.

To widen all columns:

1. Enter: / W (for *Worksheet*).

2. Key: G (for *Global*).

3. Key: C (for *Column width*).

4. Key desired width.

5. Press Enter.

To edit data already in a cell by using the Delete key:

1. Place your cell pointer in the cell to be edited.

2. Press F2 (Edit).

3. Press Home to move the pointer to the beginning of the entry line.

4. Press Del to delete all or part of the entry.

5. Key the new entry.

6. Press Enter.

To edit data already in a cell by inserting new text:

1. Move cell pointer to the cell to be edited.

2. Press F2 (Edit). Again, 1-2-3 brings the entry to the entry line.

3. Place the pointer where the insertion is to be made.

4. Complete the editing process.

To display formulas:

1. Key: / (to display the Main Menu).

2. Key: W (for *Worksheet*).

3. Key: G (for *Global*).

4. Key: F (for *Format*).

5. Key: T (for *Text*).

To turn off formulas:

1. Key: / W (for *Worksheet*).

2. Key: G (for *Global*).

3. Key: F (for *Format*).

4. Key: G (for *General*).

To insert a column or row:

1. Position your cell pointer at the location where you want to add the new row(s) or column(s).

2. Key: / (to display the Main Menu).

3. Key: W (for *Worksheet*).

4. Key: I (for *Insert*).

5. Select C (*Column*) or R (*Row*).

6. Specify the range or highlight the number of rows or columns you want to insert.

7. Press Enter.

To delete a column or row:

1. Be certain the cell pointer is in the column or row to be deleted.

2. Key: / (to display the Main Menu).

3. Key: W (for *Worksheet*).

4. Key: D (for *Delete*).

5. Choose C (*Column*) or R (*Row*).

6. Specify the range if you want to delete more than one row or column.

7. Press Enter.

To move a column:

1. Key: / W I C. Press Enter. This inserts a blank column so that you will not lose the data in the existing column.

2. Key: / (to display the Main Menu).

3. Key: M (for *Move*). The prompt reads: Enter range to move FROM:

4. Specify the FROM range.

5. Press Enter. The prompt reads: Enter range to move TO:

6. Press Enter to enter range.

7. Move cell pointer to the empty column remaining after the move to delete it.

8. Key: / W D C.

9. Specify range.

To view the format options:

1. Key: / (to display the Main Menu).

2. Key: W (for *Worksheet*).

3. Key: G (for *Global*).

4. Key: F (for *Format*). Using the right arrow, highlight the various options and read about each one in MENU mode on the Help line.

5. Press Esc until you return to READY mode.

Applications

Widen the columns where necessary. Align all labels to the right.

Application 1

View your File List and retrieve the file named SUMMARY. Use the Edit functions and the Delete key to edit the amounts in department A as shown below. Format the amounts to two decimal places.

Department A
1243.14
744.50
981.80
2620.30
423.80
5492.84

Save the file under the same name, choose Replace, and print one copy.

Application 2

Retrieve the file named HOLLOW and use F2 to edit the column named Homeowner as shown below by inserting the new text.

Homeowner
Johnson, Lee
Barrett, Joyce
Smith, Anne
Reynolds, Dianne
Green, Artie
Totals

Save the file under the same name, choose Replace, and print one copy of the file. Leave the file on your screen to use in the next application.

Application 3

Display the formulas for the file named HOLLOW. Turn off the formulas. Clear your screen.

Application 4

Retrieve the file named DPE and make the following changes:
1. Insert a blank column between City and Attendance.
2. Insert a row after Carthage, and insert Austin with 12 attending.
3. Delete the row containing the information about Tyler.
4. Delete the blank column that you created between City and Attendance.
5. Print one copy.
6. Save the file.

Application 5

Create the following spreadsheet. Complete the following instructions:
1. Enter the column headings (labels) as text.
2. Left align the labels.
3. Save and name the file RICHARDS.
4. Move the "Location" column one column to the right of the "Completion Date" column.
5. Delete the blank columns created by moving the "Location" column.
6. Save the file again, choosing Replace.
7. Compress-print one copy of the file.

GASTON RICHARDS, CONTRACTOR
Job Status Report
June 30, 19--

Job No.	Location	Completion Date
1229	Topeka, KS	02-15-90
3228	Oklahoma City, OK	01-02-90
4433	Houston, TX	06-20-90
3229	Tulsa, OK	04-15-90
1230	Kansas City, KS	01-15-90
9889	Albuquerque, NM	06-15-90
9890	Santa Fe, NM	06-15-90

5

Creating Graphics

Graphics help clarify or emphasize facts and ideas presented in business reports. That old adage, "A picture is worth a thousand words," is true. Graphs can visually help a manager make such decisions as increases in employees' salaries, ways to deal with downward trends in sales, or lowering the percentage of downtime for the company's computers. Lotus 1-2-3 has the ability to display and print five types of graphs — bar, stacked bar, line, pie, and XY line — from data saved in the spreadsheet or database.

This chapter will show you how to create and print a bar graph from your spreadsheet.

Parts of a Bar Graph

Bar graphs illustrate numerical data with bars of varying heights. Before you create your first graph, study Figure 5-1 and read the following explanations identifying the various parts of a bar graph.

The **title** is used to label the graph. You may key a one- or two-line title, which is placed at the top of the page.

Lotus 1-2-3 allows you to enter minimum and maximum numbers, which are placed on either the vertical *Y-axis* or the horizontal *X-axis*. The titles of the *X-axis* and *Y-axis* identify the information represented on each axis. You may key one line for each.

A *bar* is a block usually identified by one of a variety of shadings, colors, or grid lines.

The *legend* identifies the shadings, colors, or grid lines representing the data in each bar.

To view a graph that has already been stored on your data disk, complete the following steps.

1. Insert the 1-2-3 program disk in drive A and your data disk in drive B (A for hard disk), if they are not already there. Be certain the default directory is B (A for hard disk).

2. To retrieve the TRAVEL.WK1 spreadsheet file, key: / File Retrieve. Enter the file name. Press Enter.

3. To view the bar graph on your screen, key: / Graph View.

4. Press Enter to return to the Graph Menu.

5. Key: Q (for *Quit*) to return to READY mode.

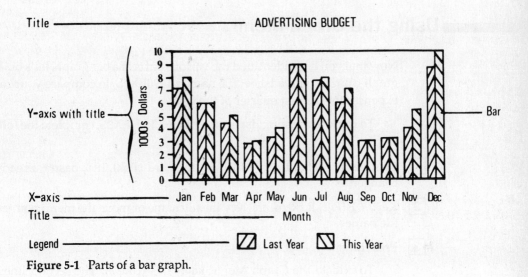

Figure 5-1 Parts of a bar graph.

6 Clear the screen (/ *Worksheet Erase Yes*).

Steps for Creating a Graph

You will learn to use the following basic steps to create a graph from a spreadsheet.

1. Load the file containing the desired spreadsheet.
2. Enter the graph command (/ Graph).
3. Key: T (Type of graph).
4. Select a graph type: B (Bar), L (Line), and so on.
5. Define the data to be included in the graph (X and A through F ranges).
6. View the graph.
7. Press Enter to return to the worksheet and the Graph Menu.
8. Name the graph with its settings.
9. Save the graph as a file.

Using the Graph Menu

Now that you have identified the various parts of a bar graph, let's build your graph from the spreadsheet file named 1990EXPS, to compare your monthly expenses for the first quarter of the year.

To retrieve the spreadsheet file named 1990EXPS, complete the following steps:

1. Change the default drive to B (A for hard disk), if it hasn't already been changed.

2. Key: / F (*File*) R (*Retrieve*). Key the file name or move the menu pointer to the file name.

3. Press Enter.

To initiate the Graph Menu, key: / G (*Graph*). The second line on the control panel displays the following Graph Menu:

```
Type X A B C D E F Reset View Save Options Name Group Quit
```

TIP: For additional information about the Graph Menu, access the Help menu and press F1. Press Esc to return to the Graph Menu.

Creating a Bar Graph

To create a bar graph, continue as follows:

1. Key: T (*Type* of graph). The second line of the panel displays the available types of graphs:

```
Line   Bar   XY   Stacked-Bar   Pie
```

2. Key: B (*Bar*). You are returned to the Graph Menu to organize the data in your graph.

Defining the *X*-Axis

The X command defines the range of the spreadsheet to be used for the horizontal axis, or X-axis. For your graph, the X-labels will be the types of expenses: Hse.Pmt., Util., and so on.

To define the X-axis, complete the following commands:

1 Key: X (*X*-axis, from the Graph Menu).

2 Enter the X-axis range B3.G3 (types of monthly expenses).

3 Press Enter.

This range sets the X-axis for your graph. Nothing appears on your screen at this point. You are returned to the Graph Menu to continue your graph settings.

Defining the Data Ranges

The ABCDEF commands on the Graph Menu allow you to specify up to six data ranges to be used in your graph. You are required to select at least one range to be used in your graph, and you must select A as the first data range.

TIP: Only the A data range is used in a pie graph. For the other graphs, the BCDEF ranges may be defined.

For your graph, you will be using four ranges: A = B5.G5 (January); B = B6.G6 (February); C = B7.G7 (March); and D = B8.G8 (April).

To select a data range from the Graph Menu, complete the following commands:

1 Key: A (first data range is January).

2 Enter first data range: B5.G5.

3 Press Enter.

4 Key: B (second data range is February).

5 Enter second data range: B6.G6.

6 Press Enter.

7 Enter the remaining data ranges, for March and April. Again, nothing appears on your screen. Leave the Graph Menu on your screen.

TIPS:

1. If you wish to cancel a data range, select the Reset option on the Graph Menu.
2. If you wish to confirm a data-range setting, key: A (the first data range should be highlighted); and press Enter. Continue by keying B, C, and so on, to confirm the remaining settings. Remember to press Enter after viewing each range.
3. You can specify all graph data ranges at once, when the X and A through F data ranges are in consecutive columns or rows in a range, by using the / Graph Group command. Press / G G, specify the group range, press Enter, then select columnwise to divide the group into data ranges by column or select rowwise to divide the group range in data by rows.

Viewing the Graph

When you use the View command, the spreadsheet is cleared from your screen, and the graph is displayed instead. To clear the graph from your screen and display the spreadsheet again, press any key.

TIP: When you are working on the graph and want to return to your spreadsheet, key Q (Quit) from the Graph Menu.

To view the graph, to see the results from entering your data ranges (A through D), complete the following steps:

1. Key: V (*View* from the Graph Menu). Your screen should look like Figure 5-2. The types of expenses are displayed on the horizontal X-axis. The amount of each expense is automatically set by 1-2-3 on the vertical Y-axis. Each bar represents a month. (The expenses on the X-axis may overlap on screen.)

2. Press Enter or any key to return to the Graph Menu.

Adding Titles to the Graph

The next step is to make your bar graph more understandable by adding some titles. The Options command lets you improve the appearance of your graph this way. By selecting the Options command from the Graph Menu, the following commands appear in the control panel:

```
Legend Format Titles Grid Scale Color B&W Data-Labels
```

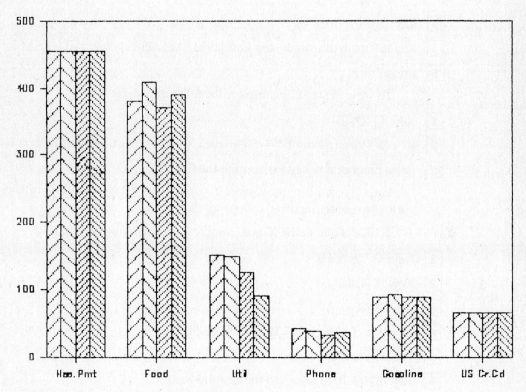

Figure 5-2 Bar graph with data ranges defined.

Lotus 1-2-3 allows you to enter a one- or two-line title at the top of the graph and a one-line title on each axis of the graph. On your graph, use 1990 EXPENSES JOHN HILL FAMILY as the first (main) title and MONTHLY EXPENSES as the X-axis title.

Use the following commands from the Graph Menu to add the first (main) title to the top of the graph:

$\boxed{1}$ Key: O (*Options*).

$\boxed{2}$ Key: T (*Titles*).

The following names appear on the control panel:

```
First     Second     X-Axis     Y-Axis
```

3 Key: F (*First* title).

4 Key the main title on the top line: 1990 EXPENSES JOHN HILL FAMILY

5 Press Enter.

To view the results, complete the following steps:

1 Key: Q (*Quit*).

2 Key: V (*View*). Lotus 1-2-3 automatically centers the title over the graph.

3 Press Enter or any key to return to the Graph Menu.

Let's give a title to the X-axis. In your graph, the X-axis title identifies the various expenses incurred every month.

To add a title to the X-axis, complete the following commands.

1 Key: O (*Options*).

2 Key: T (*Titles*).

3 Key: X (*X-axis*).

4 Key X-axis title: MONTHLY EXPENSES.

5 Press Enter.

6 Key: Q (*Quit*) to return to the Graph Menu.

7 Key: V (*View*). Your screen should show the X-axis title MONTHLY EX-PENSES at the bottom of the graph and the main title at the top of the graph.

8 Press Enter or any key to return to the Graph Menu.

Creating Legends

To distinguish among the various bars in the graph, 1-2-3 allows you to create a legend to identify the data each bar represents. Although 1-2-3 will display only 1 to 15 characters per legend, you can enter a legend label with more than 15 characters.

For your graph, you will use four legends: Jan, Feb, Mar, and Apr. To create these legends, complete the following steps:

1 Key: O (*Options*).

2 Key: L (*Legend*). The following menu is displayed:
A B C D E F Range

3 Key: A (first legend).

4 Key legend for A range: Jan (with no period at the end).

5 Press Enter.

6 Key: L (*Legend*).

7 Key: B (second legend).

8 Key legend for B range: Feb (without a period at the end).

9 Press Enter.

10 Key the remaining legends (Mar and Apr). Do not key a legend for May.

TIP: You can assign legends to all data ranges at once by using / Graph Options Legends. Press / G O L, then select the range, key the range, and press Enter.

To view the legends, use the following steps:

1 Key: Q (*Quit*).

2 Key: V (*View*). Your screen should look like Figure 5-3. The four legends that you entered via the Options/Legend Menu should be displayed at the bottom of the graph. These legends clarify the data represented by each bar.

3 Press any key to clear the graph from your screen.

Naming the Graph

A graph's settings may be saved by simply naming the graph. Using the / Graph Name command from the Graph Menu lets you save more than one graph in a spreadsheet.

To save your current graph's settings, name the graph, using the following steps:

1 Key: N (*Name*) from the Graph Menu.

The Name Menu that follows will appear in the control panel:

```
Use    Create    Delete    Reset    Table
```

2 Key: C (*Create*).

3 Key the graph name: 1990Bar. You may enter a name from 1 to 15 characters in length.

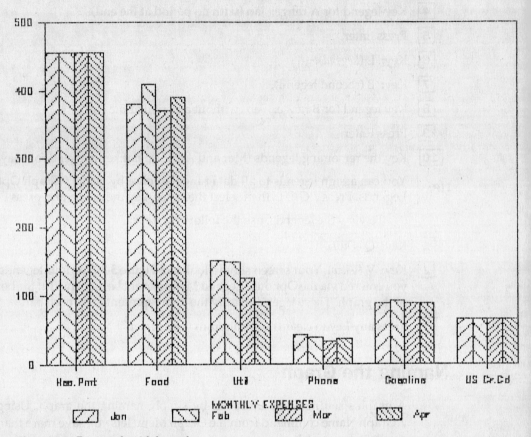

Figure 5-3 Bar graph with legends.

[4] Press Enter. You have returned to the Graph Menu.

Now that you have named your graph, you can retrieve it whenever you want to view it.

File Saving Versus Graph Savings

It is important to distinguish between saving a graph within a spreadsheet and saving a graph as a separate file.

The / File Save command saves the graph within the spreadsheet. When you retrieve the spreadsheet, the graph is there. Any changes you make in the spreadsheet are automatically carried out in the graph. You cannot print a graph when it is saved within a spreadsheet unless you also save the graph as a picture file, using the / Graph Save command.

When you save your graph as a separate file, using the / Graph Save command, the changes you make in the spreadsheet are not reflected in the graph. The / Graph Save command saves a graph only for printing with the PrintGraph program. Once the graph is saved, you cannot recall it back to the screen to modify it.

So that you can print your graph with PrintGraph, save it as follows:

1. Key: S (*Save*) from the Graph Menu.
2. Key: 1990BAR
3. Press Enter.

Your graph is saved as a picture file. Lotus 1-2-3 automatically saves the graph with the .PIC extension to distinguish the graph from the spreadsheet, which ends with a .WK file extension. The .PIC file will be displayed on the PrintGraph Menu.

Now save the graph with your spreadsheet. You are saving the graph with your spreadsheet so that any changes you make in the spreadsheet will automatically be made in the graph.

To save the graph with your spreadsheet, use the following steps:

1. Key: Q (*Quit*) from the Graph Menu.
2. Key: / File Save 1990EXPS. Select Replace.
3. To exit 1-2-3, key: / Quit Yes.

Using PrintGraph

Usually 1-2-3 provides a separate program disk to print graph files previously saved using the / Graph Save command. The name of this disk is PrintGraph.

There are six steps for printing a graph that you have created with 1-2-3:

1. Save the graph in 1-2-3 by using the / Graph Save command.
2. Load the PrintGraph program.
3. Select Settings to make any necessary changes.
4. Select Image-Select and specify the graph to be printed.

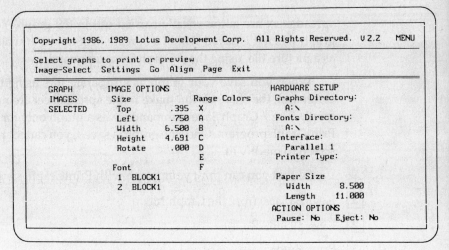

```
Copyright 1986, 1989 Lotus Development Corp.  All Rights Reserved. V 2.2   MENU

Select graphs to print or preview
Image-Select  Settings  Go  Align  Page  Exit

   GRAPH       IMAGE OPTIONS                      HARDWARE SETUP
   IMAGES      Size            Range Colors       Graphs Directory:
   SELECTED    Top        .395  X                    A:\
               Left       .750  A                 Fonts Directory:
               Width     6.500  B                    A:\
               Height    4.691  C                 Interface:
               Rotate     .000  D                    Parallel 1
                               E                  Printer Type:
               Font        F
               1  BLOCK1
               2  BLOCK1                          Paper Size
                                                     Width     8.500
                                                     Length   11.000
                                                  ACTION OPTIONS
                                                     Pause: No    Eject: No
```

Figure 5-4   PrintGraph menu.

5.   Prepare the printer to print.

6.   Select G (*Go*) to print the graph.

     Complete the following commands to load the PrintGraph program:

1   From the Access System Menu, press P to select PrintGraph (key: / Q Yes to go to the Access System Menu).

2   At the screen prompt, replace the 1-2-3 System Disk in drive A with the PrintGraph disk. If you have a hard disk, select PrintGraph from the Access System menu.

3   Press Enter. Wait for a few seconds.

     The PrintGraph Menu shown in Figure 5-4 should appear on your screen. The menu pointer should be at Image-Select.

TIP: To learn more about each of the options, move the menu pointer to each option and read the brief description on the line above the option.

     To select Settings, use the following steps:

1   Key: S (to select *Settings*).

2   Key: H (for *Hardware*).

3   Key: G (*Graphs* Directory).

4   Be sure to indicate that the graph is in the B directory or drive by keying B: (without punctuation). (For hard disk users, key: A:)

5   Press Enter. Be sure the data disk is in drive B.

6   Key: F (*Fonts* Directory); be sure to indicate that the type styles (fonts) are listed in the A directory or drive (for hard drive users, drive C).

7   Press Enter.

8   Key: Q (*Quit* Hardware Setup).

9   Key: E (*Eject*) from Action option.

10   Key: P (to select *Printer*).

11   Move the menu pointer up or down to select printer type.

12   Press Enter.

13   Key: Q (*Quit*).

     For class purpose, do not save current hardware settings.

     To select Image-Select and specify the graph to be printed, complete the following commands:

1   Key: I (Image-Select).

2   Use the up and down arrow keys to highlight your choice (1990BAR).

3   Press Enter to mark your choice. The symbol # appears in front of the graph title.

4   To view your graph before printing, press F10.

5   Press Enter to return to your selection.

6   Press Enter. Your selections have been entered and the PrintGraph Menu is displayed.

     To print the graph, complete the following commands:

1   Be sure that the printer has been prepared to print and that the paper is in the correct position.

2   Key: G (*Go*) to begin printing. It may take several seconds for printing to begin.

3   Key: E (*Exit*).

4   Key: Y (*Yes*) to end the PrintGraph session.

5   Key: 1 to select 1-2-3 from the Access Menu.

6   Replace the PrintGraph disk in drive A with the 1-2-3 System Disk.

7   Press Enter. A blank spreadsheet is displayed.

8   Change the directory to B.

TIP: You can change the type of graph without setting new data ranges. For example, if you want to see your data displayed as a stacked-bar graph, simply select and specify the graph type. Then view it.

To see how this feature works, complete the following steps:

1. Retrieve the spreadsheet file TRAVEL.

2. Key: / Graph Type

3. Key: S to change the type of graph from B (*Bar*) to S (*Stacked-Bar*).

4. Key: V (*View*) to see the stacked-bar graph.

5. Press Enter or any key to return to the Graph Menu.

6. Key: Q (to *Quit* the Graph Menu).

7. Clear the screen (/ W E Y).

Summary

To view an already stored graph:

1. Insert the 1-2-3 program disk in drive A and your data disk in drive B, if they are not already there.
2. Display the desired spreadsheet on your screen.
3. Retrieve the graph (/ File Retrieve; point to or key file name and press Enter).
4. View the graph on your screen.

To create a graph:

1. Load the file containing the desired spreadsheet.
2. Key the graph command (/ Graph).
3. Key: T (*Type* of graph).
4. Select a graph type: Key: B (*Bar*), L (*Line*), and so on.
5. Define the data to be included in the graph (X and A through F ranges).
6. View the graph.
7. Press Enter to return to the spreadsheet and the Graph Menu.
8. Name the graph.
9. Save the graph.
10. Save the file.

To define the *X*-axis (horizontal):

1. Key: X (*X*-axis, from the Graph Menu).
2. Key the *X*-axis range.
3. Press Enter.

To select a data range:

1. Key: A (first data range).
2. Key first data range.
3. Press Enter.
4. Key: B (second data range).
5. Key second data range.
6. Press Enter.
7. Continue entering the remaining data ranges. Again, nothing appears on your screen. If you wish to confirm these settings, reselect the options. The ranges should be highlighted.

To view a graph:

1. Key: V (View from the Graph Menu).
2. Press Enter or any key to return to the Graph Menu.

To add the main title to the top of the graph:

1. Key: O (*Options*).
2. Key: T (*Titles*).
3. Key: F (*First title*).
4. Key the main title for the top line.
5. Press Enter.

To add a title to the *X*-axis:

1. Key: O (*Options*).
2. Key: T (*Titles*).
3. Key: X (*X*-axis).
4. Enter X-axis title.
5. Press Enter.

To create legends:

1. Key: O (*Options*).
2. Key: L (*Legend*).
3. Key: A (first legend).
4. Key legend for A range.

5. Press Enter.

6. Key: L (*Legend*).

7. Key: B (second legend).

8. Key legend for B range.

9. Press Enter.

10. Key remaining legends.

To name a graph with its settings:

1. Key: N (*Name*) from the Graph Menu.

2. Key: C (*Create*).

3. Key the graph name. You may enter a name from 1 to 15 characters.

4. Press Enter or any key to return to the Graph Menu.

To save a graph to be printed:

1. Key: S (*Save*) from the Graph Menu.

2. Key name of graph.

3. Press Enter.

4. Save the graph as a file (/ File, Save, file name)

Steps for printing a graph:

1. Save the graph in 1-2-3 by using the / Graph Save command.

2. Load the PrintGraph program.

3. Select Settings to make any necessary changes.

4. Select Image-Select and specify the graph to be printed.

5. Prepare the printer to print.

6. Select G (*Go*) to print the graph.

To load PrintGraph:

1. From the Access System Menu, press P to select PrintGraph.

2. At the screen prompt, replace the 1-2-3 System Disk in drive A with the PrintGraph disk.

3. Press Enter.

To select settings:

1. Key: S (to select *Settings*).

2. Key: H (*Hardware*).

3. Choose the Graphs Directory.

4. Be sure to indicate that the graph is in the desired directory.

5. Press Enter.

6. Choose the Fonts Directory; be sure to indicate that the type styles (fonts) are listed in the A directory or drive (for floppy drive users).

7. Press Enter.

8. Key: E (from Action submenu).

9. Key: P (to select *Printer*).

10. Move the menu pointer up or down to select printer type.

11. Press Enter.

12. Key: Q (*Quit*).

To select Image-Select and specify the graph to be printed:

1. Press Esc until Image-Select appears.

2. Key: I to select Image-Select.

3. Use the up and down arrow keys to highlight your choice.

4. Press Enter.

To print the graph:

1. Be sure that the printer has been prepared to print and that the paper is in the correct position.

2. Key: G (*Go*) to begin printing.

3. Key: E (*Exit*).

4. Key: Y (*Yes*) to end the PrintGraph session.

5. Key: 1 to select 1-2-3 from the Access System Menu.

6. Replace the PrintGraph disk in drive A with the 1-2-3 System Disk.

7. Press Enter. A blank worksheet is displayed.

8. Change the default directory to B.

Applications

Application 1

Retrieve the file named SOFTWARE. Create a pie chart from the spreadsheet. Save the chart separately under the name SOFT. Save the spreadsheet and the pie chart as SOFTWARE. Print one graph.

1.	Purpose:	To show visually how many copies of each brand of software were sold as a percentage of the total.
2.	Main title:	DISCOUNT SOFTWARE WORLD

3.   Subtitle: Software Sales, July 19--

4.   Graph name: SOFT

Application 2

Create the following spreadsheet. Right align labels. Calculate the total snowfall. Copy the formula to calculate rainfall. Create a line graph from the
spreadsheet. Save the graph separately, naming it SNOW. Save the
spreadsheet and graph as SNOWFALL. Leave the file on your screen to use
in the next application.

WEATHER REPORT — CENTRAL PLAINS REGION
January 1 - June 30, 19--

	JAN	FEB	MAR	APR	MAY	JUN	TOTAL
Snow (feet)	6.5	7.9	3.8	1.1	.8	.05	
Rain (inches)			1.3	4.7	3.9	5.11	

---

1.   Purpose: To visually show the increases and de-
                       creases in snowfall in the Central Plains Re-
                       gion from January 1 through June 30, 19--.

2.   Main title: WEATHER REPORT——CENTRAL
                       PLAINS REGION

3.   Subtitle: January 1 - June 30, 19--

4.   Graph name: SNOW

Application 3

The file named SNOWFALL should still be on your screen. Select Reset to
cancel all data ranges. Create a bar graph to show the rainfall amounts. Check
the graph by viewing it. Save the graph separately, naming it RAIN. Save the
spreadsheet with the graph, naming the file RAINFALL. Print one graph.

1.   Purpose: To visually show the increases and de-
                       creases in rainfall in the Central Plains Re-
                       gion from January 1 through June 30, 19--.

2.   Main title: WEATHER REPORT —CENTRAL
                       PLAINS REGION

3.   Subtitle: January 1 - June 30, 19--

4.   Graph name: RAIN

Application 4

Retrieve the file named DPE and create a pie chart from the spreadsheet information. Save the pie chart as ATTEND. Save the chart and spreadsheet as DPE. Print one graph.

1.   Purpose: To visually show the attendance at the 19-- State Delta Pi Epsilon Conference by city.

2.   Main title: DELTA PI EPSILON

3.   Subtitle: 19-- State Conference

4.   Graph name: ATTEND

6

Creating and Using a Database

Most organizations already have a database, although it may not be called by that name: there are cabinets with files about customers, employees, sales, or products. People use these files to get information about the company's operations. Much of this information is kept in the form of lists, such as lists of

Personnel,
suppliers,
customers or clients,
phone numbers,
parts, or
names and addresses

A database is a collection of such lists of information, which can be stored on a floppy or hard disk drive and easily managed. For example, a personnel department could take the data collected about each employee—such as name, address, telephone number, social security number, date of hire, and salary—and enter it into a computer via 1-2-3. Lotus 1-2-3's database commands would then make it easy for the department to sort such detailed lists of data or to search through them to extract and print specific information.

Terminology

To understand database organizations, there are certain key terms you need to know.

A **file** is a collection of records and fields. For example, a file may include the personnel department's records of all employees or a small retail business's customers. A sample file is shown in Figure 6-1.

A **record** contains related information about an employee, product, or customer. A record can be compared to a file card filled with information about a customer or a product. On a spreadsheet, a record is a row of cells within the database.

A **field** is part of a record. An example of a field in a customer list may be a customer's name, address, or telephone number. A field is a column of cells within a database.

Field names are the column labels that identify categories of information. An example, shown in Figure 6-1, is ADDRESS.

Using a database allows you to sort information. If, for example, you needed to produce a mailing list to recruit students for next semester's classes, you could sort the students by time of attendance—day or evening. To refine that sorting process, you could find the addresses of those students who attended Tuesday/Thursday evening classes in the previous semester, extract their names, and print a copy of the selected records.

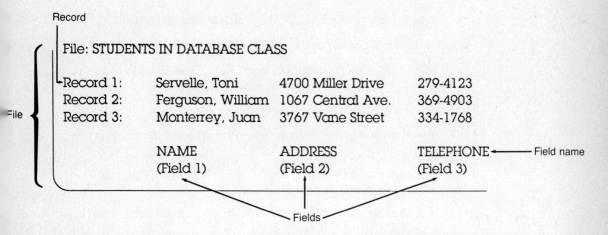

Figure 6-1 Sample file.

Viewing a Database

To view a sample database, retrieve the file named PERSNL.WK1 from your data disk, using the following steps:

[1] Key: / File (*File*) from the Main Menu.

[2] Key: R (*Retrieve*) from the Submenu.

[3] Key: PERSNL.WK1.

An example of a database should appear on your screen. The six fields (EMPLOYEE, DEPT., JOB TITLE, SERVICE DATA, NEXT REVIEW, HR. RATE) in each record are identified by the labels in row 3. The field labels are immediately followed by the first record (Robert Jackson) in cell A4 of the database. There are 7 records (A4 through A10), each occupying a row.

Revising the Database

Two types of revisions are commonly made to database files: (1) adding or deleting records (rows) or fields (columns) and (2) updating existing records.

If you want to add or delete records in a database, you use the same commands that you used earlier to insert and delete columns or rows.

Use the following steps to add or delete records (rows):

1 Move your cell pointer to the row(s) that you wish to modify.

2 To add a row, key: / Worksheet Insert Row. Press Enter to accept range. Key the new record into the new row created by the insert.

3 To delete a row, key: / Worksheet Delete Row.

4 To update existing records (rows), key the updated information directly into each cell.

5 To add a new field (column), key: / Worksheet Insert Column. Then key the new field, entering data for each record.

Let's revise a few of the records in the prepared database that appears on your screen. Use the following steps:

1 To add a row between rows A6 and A7:

    a. Place the cell pointer on cell A7.

    b. Key: / Worksheet Insert Row; press Enter.

    c. Key: Lisa McGee, Payroll, Payroll Clrk, '08-03-87, '11-10-87, "6.94. Press Enter.

2 To update Donald Lee's record, change the hourly rate from "5.82 to "6.35. Use F2 to edit the hourly rate.

3 To right-justify the column heading HR.RATE:

    a. Place the cell pointer on cell F3.

    b. Key: / Range Label Right

    c. Press Enter.

4 To save the file PERSNL:

    a. Key: / File Save.

    b. Press Enter.

    c. Select Replace.

5 To print the database:

    a. Key: / Print Printer Range.

    b. Key the range A1.F11

    c. Press Enter, Go.

6 To clear the menu, key: Q (*Quit*).

	A	B	C	D	E	F
				PERSONNEL DATABASE		
3	Employee	Dept.	Job Title	Service Date	Next Review	Hr. Rate
4	Robert Jackson	Payroll	Manager, Payroll	09-04-84	09-04-87	18.03
5	Steven Estelle	Payroll	Time/Attend Clrk	09-17-84	04-22-88	6.93
6	Cary Mason	Payroll	Payroll Clrk	06-22-83	04-24-88	8.86
7	Lisa McGee	Payroll	Payroll Clrk	08-03-87	11-10-87	6.94
8	Edyth Witaker	Payroll	Sr. Payroll Clrk	10-22-84	10-22-87	9.90
9	Susan Wong	Payroll	Payroll/Rec. Asst.	04-29-86	02-25-88	6.45
10	Carmen Lopez	Payroll	Payroll/Rec. Anal.	07-09-75	08-04-88	10.92
11	Donald Lee	Payroll	Payroll/Rec. Clrk	12-07-83	03-25-88	6.35

Figure 6-2 Records revised in database.

[7] To erase the spreadsheet, key: / Worksheet Erase Yes. (Remember that this command does not erase the file from the disk; it clears the spreadsheet from the screen.)

Now look at the revised records that you have printed. They should look like Figure 6-2.

Creating the Database

So that you can learn to work with a database, a simple employee list (listing name, address, city, state, zip code, area code, and phone number) will be used to explain the procedures in this chapter.

Before keying your spreadsheet, study the following steps to create a database:

1. Write the column labels on paper before you create the database.
2. Key a title for the database in the first row of the worksheet.
3. Key the field names, using the following rules:
    a. The database name must be entered in the first row of the database.
    b. Field names can be entered as labels or numbers.
    c. Field widths can be 1 to 240 characters.
    d. Each field name must be unique.

	A	B	C	D	E	F	G	H
1			EMPLOYEE DATABASE					
2								
3	NAME	ADDRESS	CITY	STATE	ZIP	AREA	PHONE	
4								

Figure 6-3   Field names in database.

4. Determine and key field widths for each column. Plan for the largest possible entry to that field. Key: / Worksheet Column Set Width; key the column width; press Enter.

5. Key the first record in the row immediately below the field names. You can key data across the row or vertically if you wish. Continue to key the data in the database.

6. Make necessary adjustments to improve the spreadsheet's appearance.

   a. To center the labels, key: / Range Label Center; key the range number; press Enter.

   b. To insert space between columns, key: / Worksheet Insert Column; press Enter. Then key: / Worksheet Column Set-Width; key the column width; press Enter.

7. Save and print a copy of the database.

   To create your database, complete the following steps:

1 Be sure your data disk is in drive B. Display a blank spreadsheet on your screen.

2 In cell D1, key the title EMPLOYEE DATABASE.

3 In cell A3, begin keying the field names NAME, ADDRESS, CITY, STATE, ZIP, AREA, PHONE. Your spreadsheet should look like Figure 6-3.

4 To adjust all columns to a width of 18 characters, key: / Worksheet Global Column-Width. Then key: 18. Press Enter.

5 Key the first record in cell A4, immediately below the field name. Remember to key an apostrophe before each entry in the address field.

Record 1	Record 2
Jill L. Jordan	James J. Marshall
'120 Hill St.	'9036 Audelia Dr.
Dallas TX '75222	Dallas TX '75222
'214 '6812234	'214 '3281122

Record 3
R. M. Woodard
'1015 S. Main St.
Ft. Worth TX '76110
'817 '2948192

Record 4
Mark Maloney
'2535 May Ct.
Ft. Worth TX '76112
'817 '5314848

Record 5
Marie Aloe
'2887 George St.
Dallas TX '75244
'214 '2390045

Record 6
Julie Gentry
'1424 Yucca St.
Midlothian TX '76065
'214 '7753210

Record 7
Paul Porter
'3939 Fortune Dr.
San Jose CA '95131
'408 '9424466

Record 8
David R. Moore
'1213 Graham St.
Boston MA '12108
'617 '7254589

Record 9
Betty Jones
'1212 Burr Oak
Arlington TX '76012
'817 '2778832

Record 10
Bill Hargrove
'221 Bordon Rd.
San Antonio TX '78280
'512 '4977645

6   To format your spreadsheet globally, so that labels align on the right, key: / Range Label Right. Then key: A1.G13. Press Enter. Your spreadsheet should look like Figure 6-4.

7   Save and name the file EMPLOYEE.

8   Print a copy of the database all on one page. Key the first range to print, key: L (*Line*) 6 times to insert 6 lines. Key: R (*Range*), A1.D13. Second range to print is E1.G13. Press Enter. Key: G (*Go*).

9   Key: Q (to *Quit* the Print Menu).

	A	B	C	D	E	F	G
1			EMPLOYEE DATABASE				
2							
3	NAME	ADDRESS	CITY	STATE	ZIP	AREA	PHON
4	Jill L. Jordan	120 Hill St.	Dallas	TX	75222	214	681223
5	James K. Marshall	9036 Audelia Dr.	Dallas	TX	75223	214	328112
6	R. M. Woodard	1015 S. Main St.	Ft. Worth	TX	76110	817	294819
7	Mark Maloney	2535 May Ct.	Ft. Worth	TX	76112	817	531484
8	Marie Aloe	2887 George St.	Dallas	TX	75244	214	239004
9	Julie Gentry	1424 Yacca St.	Midlothian	TX	76065	214	775321
10	Paul Porter	3939 Fortune Dr.	San Jose	CA	95131	408	942446
11	David R. Moore	1213 Graham St.	Boston	MA	12108	617	725458
12	Betty Jones	1212 Burr Oak	Arlington	TX	76012	214	277883
13	Bill Hargrove	221 Bordon Rd.	San Antonio	TX	78280	512	497764
14							
15							
16							
17							
18							
19							
20							

Figure 6-4 Database in worksheet format.

You have created the database you will be using in this chapter; however, this information is still in spreadsheet format and not yet functioning as a database. You can make it a functioning database by manipulating the data, such as sorting the records, searching for specific records, extracting or copying records, or printing certain records.

Sorting the Database

Lotus 1-2-3 lets you sort, or rearrange the sequence of, records in the database in the order you specify.

TIPS:
1. If you think you may want to refer to the original order of the records in the database, be sure to save the database before sorting it.
2. If you save the sorted database under a different name, the original database remains available for future reference.